The
Saint
Helena
Psalter

CHURCH
PUBLISHING
INCORPORATED

Library of Congress Cataloging-in-Publication Data

A record of this book is available from the Library of Congress.

Church Publishing Incorporated
19 East 34th Street
New York, NY 10016

ISBN-13: 978-1-64065-205-7 (pbk.)
ISBN-13: 978-1-64065-549-2 (ebook)

PREFACE

The process of revision of the St. Helena breviary began at the same time the Episcopal Church was revising the 1928 *Book of Common Prayer.* The Order of St. Helena and the Order of the Holy Cross had begun work together in the 1970s, and in 1976 they jointly produced *A Monastic Breviary,* which was in essence the Daily Office of the 1979 Prayer Book with additions and interpolations. This book was used in both communities until the late 1980s, when the Order of St. Helena became increasingly uncomfortable with sexist language. By 1990, the sisters had produced (but not published) a book which was a first step toward using inclusive language in their daily worship. This book was in use in all the St. Helena convents for the next ten years.

About 1998, Sister Linda Julian, working almost alone, began work on a revised Psalter, based on the *Book of Common Prayer* of 1979. She drew on resources of all kinds, especially studying other efforts to inclusivise the Psalter. Her intent was to eliminate all references to God as "he" and to greatly reduce masculine imagery, even to finding an appropriate substitute for "Lord." This first step toward the present wording of the Psalter, which was tried in the actual praying of the Office for several months, captured the imagination and won the support of the rest of the sisters. By 1999, the Chapter officially endorsed a full revision of the 1990 book, and a committee to work on it was appointed.

The committee was directed to stay as close to the Prayer Book translation of the Psalter as possible, keeping in mind the importance of being able to continue to sing the psalms in traditional monastic chant. They were well aware of the tension between following strict academic faithfulness to the original texts versus offering a freer translation or interpretation in order to make the prayer both more accessible and also reflective of contemporary worship.

Regarding text changes, the most obvious ones were those that eliminated all references to God as masculine. Wherever possible, a phrase was reworked, either avoiding a masculine pronoun for God or substituting another term, such as "Holy One" or "Mighty One," or something similar. Sometimes substituting "who" for "he," or moving from the singular to plural ("he" to "they"), offered a graceful solution. A few psalms were put into the second person, but that option was followed only as a last resort. The committee chose not to be strict about the distinction between LORD (YAHWEH) and Lord (*Adonai*) and God (*Elohim*) because of the felt need for the text to flow poetically as well as to remain singable.

There was also an attempt to eliminate other specifically masculine nouns, for example, substituting "sentries" for "watchmen," "ruler" for "prince," and "monarch" or "sovereign" for "king" (except where the king was clearly a reference to David). In addition to removing the masculine references, the committee has used alternate terms for such words as "heathen" or "alien" (which have negative connotations today), using instead "nations" or "foreigners."

The committee's work did not end with the Psalter, but also included revising the canticles, hymns, antiphons, collects, and the material used to celebrate the saints and seasons of the church year. The initial focus, however, was on the Psalms, which were prayed in their revised form in the Daily Office in every convent for several years before there was general satisfaction with the revisions. These revisions now constitute *The Saint Helena Psalter*, which the Order of St. Helena is pleased to offer to all who seek a deeper knowledge of God.

The Breviary Committee for the Psalter
Sister Cintra Pemberton, OSH, Convener
Sister Carol Andrew, OSH
Sister Ann Prentice, OSH
Sister Ellen Francis, OSH

Glory to God,
Source of all being,
Incarnate Word, and Holy Spirit, *
as it was in the beginning,
is now, and will be forever. Amen.

from the Saint Helena Breviary

Book One

Psalm 1

1 Happy are they who have not walked in the counsel of
         the wicked, *
    nor lingered in the way of sinners,
    nor sat in the seats of the scornful!

2 Their delight is in the law of the Holy One, *
    and they meditate on that law day and night.

3 They are like trees planted by streams of water,
   bearing fruit in due season, with leaves that do not wither; *
    everything they do shall prosper.

4 It is not so with the wicked; *
    they are like chaff which the wind blows away.

5 Therefore the wicked shall not stand upright when
         judgment comes *
    nor the sinner in the council of the righteous;

6 For the Holy One knows the way of the righteous, *
    but the way of the wicked is doomed.

Psalm 2

1 Why are the nations in an uproar; *
    why do the peoples mutter empty threats?

2 Why do the mighty of the earth rise up in revolt
    and the rulers plot together, *
    against God and against God's Anointed?

3 "Let us break their yoke," they say; *
    "let us cast off their bonds from us."

4 You whose throne is in heaven are laughing; *
    you have them in derision.

5 Then you speak to them in your wrath, *
    and your rage fills them with terror.

6 "I myself have set my monarch *
    upon my holy hill of Zion."

7 Let me announce the decree of God, *
    who has said to me, "You are my Son;
    this day have I begotten you.

8 Ask of me, and I will give you the nations for
        your inheritance *
    and the ends of the earth for your possession.

9 You shall crush them with an iron rod *
    and shatter them like a piece of pottery."

10 And now, you monarchs, be wise; *
    be warned, you rulers of the earth.

11 Submit to God with fear, *
    and with trembling bow before the Most High,

12 Lest God be angry and you perish, *
    for divine wrath is quickly kindled.

13 Happy are they all *
    who take refuge in God!

Psalm 3

1 O God, how many adversaries I have; *
    how many there are who rise up against me!

2 How many there are who say of me, *
    there is no help for me in my God.

3 But you, O God, are a shield about me; *
    you are my glory, the one who lifts up my head.

4 I call aloud to you, O God, *
    and you answer me from your holy hill.

5 I lie down and go to sleep; *
    I wake again, because you sustain me.

6 I do not fear the multitudes of people *
    who set themselves against me all around.

7 Rise up, O God; set me free, O my God; *
    surely, you will strike all my enemies across the face;
    you will break the teeth of the wicked.

8 Deliverance belongs to you, O Most High. *
    Your blessing be upon your people!

Psalm 4

1 Answer me when I call, O God, defender of my cause; *
    you set me free when I am hard-pressed;
    have mercy on me and hear my prayer.

2 "You mortals, how long will you dishonor my glory; *
    how long will you worship dumb idols
    and run after false gods?"

3 Know that God does wonders for the faithful; *
    when I call, God will hear me.

4 Tremble, then, and do not sin; *
    speak to your heart in silence upon your bed.

5 Offer the appointed sacrifices, *
    and put your trust in the Most High.

6 Many are saying,
    "Oh, that we might see better times!" *
    Lift up the light of your countenance upon us, O God.

7 You have put gladness in my heart, *
    more than when grain and wine and oil increase.

8 I lie down in peace; at once I fall asleep; *
    for only you, God, make me dwell in safety.

Psalm 5

1 Give ear to my words, O God; *
    consider my meditation.

2 Hearken to my cry for help, my Sovereign and my God, *
    for I make my prayer to you.

3 In the morning you hear my voice; *
    early in the morning I make my appeal and watch for you.

4 For you are not a God who takes pleasure in wickedness, *
    and evil cannot dwell with you.

5 Braggarts cannot stand in your sight; *
    you hate all those who work wickedness.

6 You destroy those who speak lies; *
    the bloodthirsty and deceitful, O God, you abhor.

7 But as for me, through the greatness of your mercy
        I will go into your house; *
    I will bow down toward your holy temple in awe of you.

8 Lead me, O God, in your righteousness,
    because of those who lie in wait for me; *
    make your way straight before me,

9 For there is no truth in their mouth; *
    there is destruction in their heart;

10 Their throat is an open grave; *
    they flatter with their tongue.

11 Declare them guilty, O God; *
    let them fall, because of their schemes.

12 Because of their many transgressions, cast them out, *
    for they have rebelled against you.

13 But all who take refuge in you will be glad; *
    they will sing out their joy for ever.

14 You will shelter them, *
    so that those who love your Name may exult in you.

15 For you, O God, will bless the righteous; *
      you will defend them with your favor as with a shield.

First Day: Evening Prayer

Psalm 6

1 O God, do not rebuke me in your anger; *
      do not punish me in your wrath.

2 Have pity on me, O God, for I am weak; *
      heal me, for my bones are racked.

3 My spirit shakes with terror; *
      how long, O God, how long?

4 Turn, O God, and deliver me; *
      save me for your mercy's sake.

5 For in death no one remembers you, *
      and who will give you thanks in the grave?

6 I grow weary because of my groaning; *
      every night I drench my bed
      and flood my couch with tears.

7 My eyes are wasted with grief *
      and worn away because of all my enemies.

8 Depart from me, all evildoers, *
      for God has heard the sound of my weeping.

9 God has heard my supplication; *
      God accepts my prayer.

10 All my enemies shall be confounded and quake with fear; *
     they shall turn back and suddenly be put to shame.

Psalm 7

1 O Most High, I take refuge in you; *
     save and deliver me from all who pursue me;

2 Lest like a lion they tear me in pieces *
     and snatch me away with none to deliver me.

3 O my God, if I have done these things: *
     if there is any wickedness in my hands,

4 If I have repaid my friend with evil *
     or plundered anyone who without cause is my enemy,

5 Then let my enemy pursue and overtake me, *
     trample my life into the ground
     and lay my honor in the dust.

6 Stand up, O God, in your wrath; *
     rise up against the fury of my enemies.

7 Awake, O my God, decree justice; *
     let the assembly of the peoples gather round you.

8 Be seated on your lofty throne, O Most High; *
     O God, judge the nations.

9 Give judgment for me according to my
             righteousness, O God, *
     and according to my innocence, O Most High.

10 Let the malice of the wicked come to an end,
    but establish the righteous, *
        for you test the mind and heart, O righteous God.

11 God is my shield and defense, *
    the savior of the true in heart.

12 God is a righteous judge, *
    who sits in judgment every day.

13 If they will not repent, God will whet a sword, *
    bend a bow and make it ready.

14 God has prepared the weapons of death *
    and has made arrows shafts of fire.

15 Look at those who are in labor with wickedness, *
    who conceive evil, and give birth to a lie.

16 They dig a pit and make it deep *
    and fall into the hole that they have made.

17 Their malice turns back upon their own head; *
    their violence falls on their own scalp.

18 I will bear witness that God is righteous; *
    I will praise the Name of the Most High.

PSALM 8

1 O God, our Governor, *
    how exalted is your Name in all the world!

2 Out of the mouths of infants and children, *
    your majesty is praised above the heavens.

3 You have set up a stronghold against your adversaries, *
    to quell the enemy and the avenger.

4 When I consider your heavens, the work of your fingers, *
    the moon and the stars you have set in their courses,

5 What are we that you should be mindful of us, *
    mere mortals that you should seek us out?

6 You have made us but little lower than the angels; *
    you adorn us with glory and honor;

7 You give us mastery over the works of your hands; *
    you put all things under our feet:

8 All sheep and oxen, *
    even the wild beasts of the field,

9 The birds of the air, the fish of the sea, *
    and whatsoever walks in the paths of the sea.

10 O God, our Governor, *
    how exalted is your Name in all the world!

Second Day: Morning Prayer

PSALM 9

1 I will give thanks to you, O God, with my whole heart; *
    I will tell of all your marvelous works.

2 I will be glad and rejoice in you; *
    I will sing to your Name, O Most High.

3 When my enemies are driven back, *
    they will stumble and perish at your presence.

4 For you have maintained my right and my cause; *
    you sit upon your throne judging right.

5 You have rebuked the ungodly and destroyed the wicked; *
    you have blotted out their name for ever and ever.

6 As for the enemy, they are finished, in perpetual ruin, *
    their cities plowed under, the memory of them perished;

7 But you, O God, are enthroned for ever; *
    you have set up your throne for judgment.

8 You rule the world with righteousness *
    and judge the peoples with equity.

9 You will be a refuge for the oppressed, *
    a refuge in time of trouble.

10 Those who know your Name will put their trust in you, *
    for you never forsake those who seek you, O God.

11 Sing praise to the Holy One who dwells in Zion; *
    proclaim to the peoples the things God has done.

12 The Avenger of blood will remember them *
    and will not forget the cry of the afflicted.

13 Have pity on me, O God; *
    see the misery I suffer from those who hate me,
    O you who lift me up from the gate of death,

14 So that I may tell of all your praises
    and rejoice in your salvation *
    in the gates of the city of Zion.

15 The ungodly have fallen into the pit they dug, *
    and in the snare they set is their own foot caught.

16 You are known, O God, by your acts of justice; *
    the wicked are trapped in the works of their own hands.

17 The wicked shall be given over to the grave *
    and also all the peoples that forget God.

18 For the needy shall not always be forgotten, *
    and the hope of the poor shall not perish for ever.

19 Rise up, O God; let not the ungodly have the upper hand; *
    let them be judged before you.

20 Put fear upon them, O God; *
    let the ungodly know they are but mortal.

PSALM 10

1 Why do you stand so far off, O God, *
    and hide yourself in time of trouble?

2 The wicked arrogantly persecute the poor, *
    but they are trapped in the schemes they have devised.

3 The wicked boast of their heart's desire; *
    the covetous curse and revile God.

4 The wicked are so proud that they care not for God; *
    their only thought is, "God does not matter."

5 Their ways are devious at all times;
    your judgments are far above out of their sight; *
    they defy all their enemies.

6 They say in their heart, "I shall not be shaken; *
    no harm shall happen to me ever."

7 Their mouth is full of cursing, deceit, and oppression; *
   under their tongue are mischief and wrong.

8 They lurk in ambush in public squares,
   and in secret places they murder the innocent; *
     they spy out the helpless.

9 They lie in wait, like a lion in a covert;
   they lie in wait to seize upon the lowly; *
     they seize the lowly and drag them away in their net.

10 The innocent are broken and humbled before them; *
     the helpless fall before their power.

11 They say in their heart, "God has forgotten; *
     God has looked away and will never notice."

12 Rise up, O Holy One;
   lift up your hand, O God; *
     do not forget the afflicted.

13 Why should the wicked revile God; *
     why should they say in their heart, "You do not care"?

14 Surely, you behold trouble and misery; *
     you see it and take it into your own hand.

15 The helpless commit themselves to you, *
     for you are the helper of orphans.

16 Break the power of the wicked and evil; *
     search out their wickedness until you find none.

17 God is sovereign for ever and ever; *
     the ungodly shall perish from the land.

18 God will hear the desire of the humble; *
    you will strengthen their heart and your ears shall hear,

19 To give justice to the orphan and oppressed, *
    so that mere mortals may strike terror no more.

Psalm 11

1 In God have I taken refuge; *
    how then can you say to me,
    "Fly away like a bird to the hilltop,

2 For see how the wicked bend the bow
  and fit their arrows to the string, *
    to shoot from ambush at the true of heart.

3 When the foundations are being destroyed, *
    what can the righteous do?"

4 You, O God, are in your holy temple; *
    your throne is in heaven.

5 Your eyes behold the inhabited world; *
    your piercing eye weighs our worth.

6 You weigh the righteous as well as the wicked, *
    but those who delight in violence you abhor.

7 Upon the wicked you shall rain coals of fire
      and burning sulfur; *
    a scorching wind shall be their lot.

8 For you are righteous;
  you delight in righteous deeds, *
    and the just shall see your face.

PSALM 12

1 Help me, O God, for there is no godly one left; *
   the faithful have vanished from among us.

2 They all speak falsely with their neighbors; *
   with a smooth tongue they speak from a double heart.

3 Oh, that God would cut off all smooth tongues *
   and close the lips that utter proud boasts!

4 Those who say, "With our tongue will we prevail; *
   our lips are our own; who is ruler over us?"

5 "Because the needy are oppressed,
   and the poor cry out in misery, *
      I will rise up," says God,
      "and give them the help they long for."

6 The words of God are pure words, *
   like silver refined from ore
   and purified seven times in the fire.

7 O God, watch over us *
   and save us from this generation for ever.

8 The wicked prowl on every side, *
   and that which is worthless is highly prized by everyone.

PSALM 13

1 How long, O God?
   Will you forget me for ever; *
      how long will you hide your face from me?

2 How long shall I have perplexity in my mind
   and grief in my heart, day after day; *
      how long shall my enemy triumph over me?

3 Look upon me and answer me, O God, my God; *
      give light to my eyes, lest I sleep in death;

4 Lest my enemies say they have prevailed over me, *
      and my foes rejoice that I have fallen.

5 But I put my trust in your mercy; *
      my heart is joyful because of your saving help.

6 I will sing to the Holy One, who has dealt with me richly; *
      I will praise the Name of God Most High.

Psalm 14

1 The foolish have said in their hearts, "There is no God." *
      All are corrupt and commit abominable acts;
      there is none who does any good.

2 The Holy One looks down from heaven upon us all, *
      to see if there is any who is wise,
      if there is one who seeks after God.

3 Every one has proved faithless;
   all alike have turned bad; *
      there is none who does good; no, not one.

4 Have they no knowledge, all those evildoers *
      who eat up my people like bread
      and do not call upon God?

5 See how they tremble with fear, *
     because God is in the company of the righteous.

6 Their aim is to confound the plans of the afflicted, *
     but God is their refuge.

7 Oh, that Israel's deliverance would come out of Zion! *
     When God restores the fortunes of the people,
     Jacob will rejoice and Israel be glad.

Third Day: Morning Prayer

PSALM 15

1 O God, who may dwell in your tabernacle; *
     who may abide upon your holy hill?

2 Those who lead blameless lives and do what is right, *
     who speak truthfully from the heart.

3 There is no guile upon their tongues;
   they do no evil to their friends; *
     they do not heap contempt upon their neighbors;

4 In their sight the wicked are rejected, *
     but they honor those who fear God.

5 They have sworn to do no wrong *
     and do not take back their word.

6 They do not give their money in hope of gain, *
     nor do they take a bribe against the innocent.

7 Whoever does these things *
     shall never be overthrown.

Psalm 16

1 Protect me, O God, for I take refuge in you; *
   I have said to the Holy One, "You are my God,
   my good above all other."

2 All my delight is upon the godly that are in the land, *
   upon those who are noble among the people.

3 But those who run after other gods *
   shall have their troubles multiplied.

4 Their libations of blood I will not offer, *
   nor take the names of their gods upon my lips.

5 O God, you are my portion and my cup; *
   it is you who uphold my lot.

6 My boundaries enclose a pleasant land; *
   indeed, I have a goodly heritage.

7 I will bless you, O God who gives me counsel; *
   my heart teaches me, night after night.

8 I have set you always before me; *
   because you are at my right hand I shall not fall.

9 My heart, therefore, is glad and my spirit rejoices; *
   my body also shall rest in hope.

10 For you will not abandon me to the grave, *
   nor let your holy one see the Pit.

11 You will show me the path of life; *
   in your presence there is fullness of joy,
   and in your right hand are pleasures for evermore.

PSALM 17

1 Hear my plea of innocence, O God;
  give heed to my cry; *
    listen to my prayer, which does not come from lying lips.

2 Let my vindication come forth from your presence; *
  let your eyes be fixed on justice.

3 Weigh my heart, summon me by night, *
  melt me down; you will find no impurity in me.

4 I give no offense with my mouth as others do; *
  I have heeded the words of your lips.

5 My footsteps hold fast to the ways of your law; *
  in your paths my feet shall not stumble.

6 I call upon you, O God, for you will answer me; *
  incline your ear to me and hear my words.

7 Show me your marvelous loving-kindness, *
  O Savior of those who take refuge at your right hand
  from those who rise up against them.

8 Keep me as the apple of your eye; *
  hide me under the shadow of your wings,

9 From the wicked who assault me, *
  from my deadly enemies who surround me.

10 They have closed their heart to pity, *
  and their mouth speaks proud things.

11 They press me hard,
  now they surround me, *
    watching how they may cast me to the ground,

12 Like a lion, greedy for its prey, *
    and like a young lion lurking in secret places.

13 Arise, O God; confront them and bring them down; *
    deliver me from the wicked by your sword.

14 Deliver me, O God, by your hand, *
    from those whose portion in life is this world;

15 Whose bellies you fill with your treasure; *
    who are well supplied with children
    and leave their wealth to their little ones.

16 But at my vindication I shall see your face; *
    when I awake, I shall be satisfied, beholding your likeness.

Third Day: Evening Prayer

PSALM 18

PART I

1 I love you, O God, my strength, *
    my stronghold, my crag, and my haven,

2 My God, my rock in whom I put my trust, *
    my shield, the horn of my salvation, and my refuge;
    you are worthy of praise.

3 I will call upon you, O God, *
    and so shall I be saved from my enemies.

4 The breakers of death rolled over me, *
    and the torrents of oblivion made me afraid.

5 The cords of hell entangled me, *
    and the snares of death were set for me.

6 I called upon you, O God, in my distress; *
    I cried out to you for help.

7 You heard my voice from your heavenly dwelling; *
    my cry of anguish came to your ears.

8 The earth reeled and rocked; *
    the roots of the mountains shook;
    they reeled because of your anger.

9 Smoke rose from your nostrils
    and a consuming fire out of your mouth; *
    hot burning coals blazed forth from you.

10 You parted the heavens and came down *
    with a storm cloud under your feet.

11 You mounted on cherubim and flew; *
    you swooped on the wings of the wind.

12 You wrapped darkness about you; *
    you made dark waters and thick clouds your pavilion.

13 From the brightness of your presence, through the clouds, *
    burst hailstones and coals of fire.

14 O God, you thundered out of heaven; *
    O Most High, you uttered your voice.

15 You loosed your arrows and scattered them; *
    you hurled thunderbolts and routed them.

16 The beds of the seas were uncovered,
   and the foundations of the world laid bare, *
     at your battle cry, O God,
     at the blast of the breath of your nostrils.

17 You reached down from on high and grasped me; *
     you drew me out of great waters.

18 You delivered me from my strong enemies
   and from those who hated me, *
     for they were too mighty for me.

19 They confronted me in the day of my disaster, *
     but you were my support.

20 You brought me out into an open place; *
     you rescued me because you delighted in me.

PSALM 18: PART II

21 You rewarded me because of my righteous dealing; *
     because my hands were clean you rewarded me;

22 For I have kept your ways, O God, *
     and have not offended against you;

23 For all your judgments are before my eyes, *
     and your decrees I have not put away from me;

24 For I have been blameless with you *
     and have kept myself from iniquity;

25 Therefore you rewarded me according to my
           righteous dealing, *
     because of the cleanness of my hands in your sight.

26 With the faithful you show yourself faithful, O God; *
     with the forthright you show yourself forthright.

27 With the pure you show yourself pure, *
     but with the crooked you are wily.

28 You will save a lowly people, *
     but you will humble the haughty eyes.

29 You, O God, are my lamp; *
     my God, you make my darkness bright.

30 With you I will break down an enclosure; *
     with the help of my God I will scale any wall.

31 O God, your ways are perfect;
   your words are tried in the fire; *
     you are a shield to all who trust in you.

32 For who is God but you, O Holy One; *
     who is the Rock, except you, our God?

33 It is you who gird me about with strength *
     and make my way secure.

34 You make me sure-footed like a deer *
     and let me stand firm on the heights.

35 You train my hands for battle *
     and my arms for bending even a bow of bronze.

36 You have given me your shield of victory; *
     your right hand also sustains me;
     your loving care makes me great.

37 You lengthen my stride beneath me, *
     and my ankles do not give way.

38 I pursue my enemies and overtake them; *
    I will not turn back till I have destroyed them.

39 I strike them down, and they cannot rise; *
    they fall defeated at my feet.

40 You have girded me with strength for the battle; *
    you have cast down my adversaries beneath me;
    you have put my enemies to flight.

41 I destroy those who hate me;
    they cry out, but there is none to help them; *
    they cry to you, O God, but you do not answer.

42 I beat them small like dust before the wind; *
    I trample them like mud in the streets.

43 You deliver me from the strife of the peoples; *
    you put me at the head of the nations.

44 A people I have not known shall serve me;
    no sooner shall they hear than they shall obey me; *
    strangers will cringe before me.

45 The foreign peoples will lose heart; *
    they shall come trembling out of their strongholds.

46 You live, O God! You, my Rock, are blest; *
    exalted are you, O God of my salvation!

47 You are the one who gave me victory *
    and cast down the peoples beneath me.

48 You rescued me from the fury of my enemies;
    you exalted me above those who rose against me; *
    you saved me from my deadly foe.

49 Therefore will I extol you among the nations, O God, *
    and sing praises to your Name.

50 You multiply the victories of your king; *
    you show loving-kindness to your anointed,
    to David and his descendants for ever.

Fourth Day: Morning Prayer

PSALM 19

1 The heavens declare your glory, O God, *
    and the firmament shows your handiwork.

2 One day tells its tale to another, *
    and one night imparts knowledge to another.

3 Although they have no words or language, *
    and their voices are not heard,

4 Their sound has gone out into all lands, *
    and their message to the ends of the world.

5 In the deep you have set a pavilion for the sun; *
    it comes forth like a bridegroom out of his chamber;
    it rejoices like a champion to run its course.

6 It goes forth from the uttermost edge of the heavens
    and runs about to the end of it again; *
    nothing is hidden from its burning heat.

7 Your law, O God, is perfect and revives the soul; *
    your testimony is sure and gives wisdom to the innocent.

8 Your statutes are just and rejoice the heart; *
    your commandment is clear and gives light to the eyes.

9 The fear of you is clean and endures for ever; *
    your judgments are true and righteous altogether.

10 More to be desired are they than gold,
        more than much fine gold; *
    sweeter far than honey, than honey in the comb.

11 By them also is your servant enlightened, *
    and in keeping them there is great reward.

12 Who can tell how often one offends? *
    Cleanse me from my secret faults.

13 Above all, keep your servant from presumptuous sins;
    let them not get dominion over me; *
        then shall I be whole and sound,
        and innocent of a great offense.

14 Let the words of my mouth and the meditation of my
        heart be acceptable in your sight, *
    O God, my strength and my redeemer.

Psalm 20

1 May the Most High answer you in the day of trouble, *
    the Name of the God of Jacob defend you;

2 Send you help from the holy place *
    and strengthen you out of Zion;

3 Remember all your offerings *
    and accept your burnt sacrifice;

4 Grant you your heart's desire *
   and prosper all your plans.

5 We will shout for joy at your victory
   and triumph in the Name of our God; *
      may the Most High grant all your requests.

6 Now I know that God gives victory to the anointed one; *
   out of the holy heaven God will answer,
      with a strong and victorious right hand.

7 Some put their trust in chariots and some in horses, *
   but we will call upon the Name of our God.

8 They collapse and fall down, *
   but we will arise and stand upright.

9 O God, give victory to our sovereign, *
   and answer us when we call.

Psalm 21

1 The king rejoices in your strength, O God; *
   how greatly he exults in your victory!

2 You have given him his heart's desire; *
   you have not denied him the request of his lips,

3 For you meet him with blessings of prosperity *
   and set a crown of fine gold upon his head.

4 He asked you for life, and you gave it to him: *
   length of days, for ever and ever.

5 His honor is great, because of your victory; *
   splendor and majesty have you bestowed upon him.

6 For you will give him everlasting felicity *
    and will make him glad with the joy of your presence.

7 For the king puts his trust in God; *
    because of the loving-kindness of the Most High,
        he will not fall.

8 Your hand will lay hold upon all your enemies; *
    your right hand will seize all those who hate you.

9 You will make them like a fiery furnace *
    at the time of your appearing, O God.

10 You will swallow them up in your wrath, *
    and fire shall consume them.

11 You will destroy their offspring from the land *
    and their descendants from among the peoples of the earth.

12 Though they intend evil against you
  and devise wicked schemes, *
    yet they shall not prevail.

13 For you will put them to flight *
    and aim your arrows at them.

14 Be exalted, O God, in your might; *
    we will sing and praise your power.

PSALM 22

1 My God, my God, why have you forsaken me, *
    and are so far from my cry
    and from the words of my distress?

2 O my God, I cry in the daytime, but you do not answer; *
    by night as well, but I find no rest.

3 Yet you are the Holy One, *
    enthroned upon the praises of Israel.

4 Our forebears put their trust in you; *
    they trusted, and you delivered them.

5 They cried out to you and were delivered; *
    they trusted in you and were not put to shame.

6 But as for me, I am a worm, and less than human, *
    scorned by all and despised by the people.

7 All who see me laugh me to scorn; *
    they curl their lips and wag their heads, saying,

8 "You trusted in God for deliverance; *
    let God rescue you, if God delights in you."

9 Yet you, O God, are the one who took me out of the womb *
    and kept me safe upon my mother's breast.

10 I have been entrusted to you ever since I was born; *
    you were my God when I was still in my mother's womb.

11 Be not far from me, for trouble is near, *
    and there is none to help.

12 Many young bulls encircle me; *
     strong bulls of Bashan surround me.

13 They open wide their jaws at me, *
     like a ravening and a roaring lion.

14 I am poured out like water;
   all my bones are out of joint; *
     my heart within my breast is melting wax.

15 My mouth is dried out like a pot-sherd;
   my tongue sticks to the roof of my mouth, *
     and you have laid me in the dust of the grave.

16 Packs of dogs close me in,
   and gangs of evildoers circle around me; *
     they pierce my hands and my feet;
     I can count all my bones.

17 They stare and gloat over me; *
     they divide my garments among them;
     they cast lots for my clothing.

18 Be not far away, O God; *
     you are my strength; hasten to help me.

19 Save me from the sword, *
     my life from the power of the dog.

20 Save me from the lion's mouth, *
     my wretched body from the horns of wild bulls.

21 I will declare your Name to my people; *
     In the midst of the congregation I will praise you.

22 May all who fear you, O God, give praise; *
    may the offspring of Israel stand in awe
    and all of Jacob's line give glory.

23 For you do not despise nor abhor the poor in their poverty,
    neither do you hide your face from them, *
        but when they cry to you, you hear them.

24 My praise is of you in the great assembly; *
    I will perform my vows in the presence of those who
        worship you.

25 The poor shall eat and be satisfied,
    and those who seek you shall praise you: *
        "May your heart live for ever!"

26 All the ends of the earth shall remember and turn to you, *
    and all the families of the nations shall bow before you.

27 For yours is the royal power, O God; *
    you rule over the nations.

28 To you alone all who sleep in the earth bow down
        in worship; *
    all who go down to the dust fall before you.

29 My soul shall live for you;
    my descendants shall serve you; *
        they shall be known as yours for ever.

30 They shall come and make known to a people yet unborn *
    the saving deeds that you have done.

Psalm 23

1 O God, you are my shepherd; *
   I shall not be in want.

2 You make me lie down in green pastures *
   and lead me beside still waters.

3 You revive my soul *
   and guide me along right pathways
      for the sake of your Name.

4 Though I walk through the valley of the shadow of death,
   I shall fear no evil, *
      for you are with me;
      your rod and your staff, they comfort me.

5 You spread a table before me in the presence of those
      who trouble me; *
      you have anointed my head with oil,
      and my cup is running over.

6 Surely your goodness and mercy shall follow me
      all the days of my life, *
      and I will dwell in the house of God for ever.

Fifth Day: Morning Prayer

Psalm 24

1 The earth is God's and all that is in it, *
   the world and all who dwell therein.

2 For it is God who founded it upon the seas *
   and made it firm upon the rivers of the deep.

3 "Who can ascend the hill of the Most High, *
   and who can stand in God's holy place?"

4 "Those who have clean hands and a pure heart, *
   who have not pledged themselves to falsehood
   nor sworn by what is a fraud.

5 They shall receive a blessing from the Holy One *
   and a just reward from the God of their salvation."

6 Such is the generation of those who seek God, *
   of those who seek your face, O God of Jacob.

7 Lift up your heads, O gates;
   lift them high, O everlasting doors, *
   and the One who reigns in glory shall come in.

8 "Who is this who reigns in glory?" *
   "The Holy One, strong and mighty,
   the Holy One, mighty in battle."

9 Lift up your heads, O gates;
   lift them high, O everlasting doors, *
   and the One who reigns in glory shall come in.

10 "Who is this who reigns in glory?" *
   "This is God, the God of hosts,
   who reigns in glory."

PSALM 25

1 To you, O God, I lift up my soul;
   my God, I put my trust in you; *
   let me not be humiliated,
   nor let my enemies triumph over me.

2 Let none who look to you be put to shame; *
　　let the treacherous be disappointed in their schemes.

3 Show me your ways, O God, *
　　and teach me your paths.

4 Lead me in your truth and teach me, *
　　for you are the God of my salvation;
　　in you have I trusted all the day long.

5 Remember, O God, your compassion and love, *
　　for they are from everlasting.

6 Remember not the sins of my youth and my transgressions; *
　　remember me according to your love
　　and for the sake of your goodness, O God.

7 Gracious and upright are you; *
　　therefore you teach sinners in your way.

8 You guide the humble in doing right *
　　and teach your way to the lowly.

9 All your paths are love and faithfulness *
　　to those who keep your covenant and your testimonies.

10 For your Name's sake, O God, *
　　forgive my sin, for it is great.

11 Who are they who fear you? *
　　You will teach them the way that they should choose.

12 They shall dwell in prosperity, *
　　and their offspring shall inherit the land.

13 You are a friend to those who fear you *
　　and will show them your covenant.

14 My eyes are ever looking to you, *
     for you shall pluck my feet out of the net.

15 Turn to me and have pity on me, *
     for I am left alone and in misery.

16 The sorrows of my heart have increased; *
     bring me out of my troubles.

17 Look upon my adversity and misery, *
     and forgive me all my sin.

18 Look upon my enemies, for they are many, *
     and they bear a violent hatred against me.

19 Protect my life and deliver me; *
     let me not be put to shame, for I have trusted in you.

20 Let integrity and uprightness preserve me, *
     for my hope has been in you.

21 Deliver the people of Israel, O God, *
     out of all their troubles.

Psalm 26

1 Give judgment for me, O God,
     for I have lived with integrity; *
        I have trusted in you and have not faltered.

2 Test me, O God, and try me; *
     examine my heart and my mind.

3 For your love is before my eyes; *
     I have walked faithfully with you.

4 I have not sat with the worthless, *
  nor do I consort with the deceitful.

5 I have hated the company of evildoers; *
  I will not sit down with the wicked.

6 I will wash my hands in innocence, O God, *
  that I may go in procession round your altar,

7 Singing aloud a song of thanksgiving *
  and recounting all your wonderful deeds.

8 O God, I love the house in which you dwell *
  and the place where your glory abides.

9 Do not sweep me away with sinners *
  nor my life with those who thirst for blood,

10 Whose hands are full of evil plots *
  and their right hand full of bribes.

11 As for me, I will live with integrity; *
  redeem me, O God, and have pity on me.

12 My foot stands on level ground; *
  in the full assembly I will bless you, O God.

Fifth Day: Evening Prayer

PSALM 27

1 God is my light and my salvation;
  whom then shall I fear? *
    God is the strength of my life;
    of whom then shall I be afraid?

2 When evildoers came upon me to eat up my flesh, *
    it was they, my foes and my adversaries,
        who stumbled and fell.

3 Though an army should encamp against me, *
    yet my heart shall not be afraid;

4 And though war should rise up against me, *
    yet will I put my trust in God.

5 One thing have I asked of you, O God;
  one thing I seek: *
    that I may dwell in your house all the days of my life,

6 To behold your fair beauty, O God, *
    and to seek you in your temple.

7 For in the day of trouble you shall keep
        me safe in your shelter; *
    you shall hide me in the secrecy of your dwelling
    and set me high upon a rock.

8 Even now you lift up my head *
    above my enemies round about me.

9 Therefore I will offer in your dwelling an oblation
  with sounds of great gladness; *
    I will sing and make music to you.

10 Hearken to my voice, O Most High, when I call; *
    have mercy on me and answer me.

11 You speak in my heart and say, "Seek my face." *
    Your face, O God, will I seek.

12 Hide not your face from me, *
      nor turn away your servant in displeasure.

13 You have been my helper;
    cast me not away; *
      do not forsake me, O God of my salvation.

14 Though my father and my mother forsake me, *
      you will sustain me.

15 Show me your way, O God; *
      lead me on a level path, because of my enemies.

16 Deliver me not into the hand of my adversaries, *
      for false witnesses have risen up against me
      and also those who speak malice.

17 What if I had not believed
    that I should see the goodness of my God *
      in the land of the living!

18 O tarry and await God's pleasure;
    be strong, and let your heart take comfort; *
      wait patiently for God.

Psalm 28

1 O God, I call to you;
    my Rock, do not be deaf to my cry; *
      lest, if you do not hear me,
      I become like those who go down to the Pit.

2 Hear the voice of my prayer when I cry out to you, *
      when I lift up my hands to your holy of holies.

3 Do not snatch me away with the wicked or with
      the evildoers, *
   who speak peaceably with their neighbors,
   while strife is in their hearts.

4 Repay them according to their deeds, *
   and according to the wickedness of their actions.

5 According to the work of their hands repay them, *
   and give them their just deserts.

6 They have no understanding of your doings
   nor of the works of your hands; *
      therefore you will break them down and
         not build them up.

7 Blest are you, O God, *
   for you have heard the voice of my prayer.

8 You are my strength and my shield; *
   my heart trusts in you, and I have been helped;

9 Therefore my heart dances for joy, *
   and in my song will I praise you.

10 You are the strength of your people, *
    a safe refuge for your anointed.

11 Save your people and bless your inheritance; *
    shepherd them and carry them for ever.

PSALM 29

1 Ascribe to God, you heavenly beings, *
   ascribe to God glory and strength.

2 Ascribe due honor to God's holy Name; *
   worship the Most High in the beauty of holiness.

3 The voice of God is upon the waters;
  the God of glory thunders; *
   God is upon the mighty waters.

4 The voice of God is a powerful voice; *
   the voice of God is a voice of splendor.

5 The voice of God breaks the cedar trees; *
   God breaks the cedars of Lebanon;

6 God makes Lebanon skip like a calf *
   and Mount Hermon like a young wild ox.

7 The voice of God splits the flames of fire;
  the voice of God shakes the wilderness; *
   God shakes the wilderness of Kadesh.

8 The voice of God makes the oak trees writhe *
   and strips the forests bare.

9 And in the temple of the Holy One, *
   all are crying, "Glory!"

10 God sits enthroned above the flood, *
   enthroned as Sovereign for evermore.

11 God shall give strength to the people; *
   God shall give the people the blessing of peace.

PSALM 30

1 I will exalt you, O God,
     because you have lifted me up *
          and have not let my enemies triumph over me.

2 O my God, I cried out to you, *
     and you restored me to health.

3 You brought me up, O God, from the dead; *
     you restored my life as I was going down to the grave.

4 Sing to God, you servants of God, *
     and give thanks for the remembrance of God's holiness.

5 For divine wrath endures but the twinkling of an eye, *
     divine favor for a lifetime.

6 Weeping may spend the night, *
     but joy comes in the morning.

7 While I felt secure, I said,
     "I shall never be disturbed. *
          You, O God, with your favor, made me as strong as
               the mountains."

8 Then you hid your face, *
     and I was filled with fear.

9 I cried to you, O God; *
     I pleaded with you, saying,

10 "What profit is there in my blood, if I go down to the Pit; *
     will the dust praise you or declare your faithfulness?

11 Hear, O God, and have mercy upon me; *
    O God, be my helper."

12 You have turned my wailing into dancing; *
    you have put off my sack-cloth and clothed me with joy.

13 Therefore my heart sings to you without ceasing; *
    O God, my God, I will give you thanks for ever.

Psalm 31

1 In you, O God, have I taken refuge;
  let me never be put to shame; *
    deliver me in your righteousness.

2 Incline your ear to me; *
    make haste to deliver me.

3 Be my strong rock, a castle to keep me safe,
  for you are my crag and my stronghold; *
    for the sake of your Name, lead me and guide me.

4 Take me out of the net that they have secretly set for me, *
    for you are my tower of strength.

5 Into your hands I commend my spirit, *
    for you have redeemed me, O God of truth.

6 I hate those who cling to worthless idols, *
    and I put my trust in God.

7 I will rejoice and be glad because of your mercy, *
    for you have seen my affliction;
    you know my distress.

8 You have not shut me up in the power of the enemy; *
    you have set my feet in an open place.

9 Have mercy on me, O God, for I am in trouble; *
    my eye is consumed with sorrow,
    and also my throat and my belly.

10 For my life is wasted with grief
    and my years with sighing; *
        my strength fails me because of affliction,
        and my bones are consumed.

11 I have become a reproach to all my enemies and
            even to my neighbors,
    a dismay to those of my acquaintance; *
        when they see me in the street they avoid me.

12 I am forgotten like the dead, out of mind; *
    I am as useless as a broken pot.

13 For I have heard the whispering of the crowd;
    fear is all around; *
        they put their heads together against me;
        they plot to take my life.

14 But as for me, I have trusted in you, O God. *
    I have said, "You are my God.

15 My times are in your hand; *
    rescue me from the hand of my enemies
    and from those who persecute me.

16 Make your face to shine upon your servant, *
    and in your loving-kindness, save me."

17 O God, let me not be ashamed for having called upon you; *
    rather, let the wicked be put to shame;
    let them be silent in the grave.

18 Let the lying lips be silenced which speak against
         the righteous, *
    haughtily, disdainfully, and with contempt.

19 How great is your goodness, O God,
  which you have laid up for those who fear you, *
    which you have done in the sight of all
    for those who put their trust in you.

20 You hide them in the covert of your presence from those
         who slander them; *
    you keep them in your shelter from the strife of tongues.

21 Blessed be God! *
    For you have shown me the wonders of your love
         in a city under siege.

22 Yet I said in my alarm,
  "I have been cut off from the sight of your eyes." *
    Nevertheless, you heard the sound of my entreaty
    when I cried out to you.

23 Love God, all you who worship God; *
    God protects the faithful,
    but repays to the full those who act haughtily.

24 Be strong and let your heart take courage, *
    all you who wait for God.

Psalm 32

1 Happy are they whose transgressions are forgiven *
   and whose sin is put away!

2 Happy are they to whom God imputes no guilt *
   and in whose spirit there is no guile!

3 While I held my tongue, my bones withered away, *
   because of my groaning all day long.

4 For your hand was heavy upon me day and night; *
   my moisture was dried up as in the heat of summer.

5 Then I acknowledged my sin to you *
   and did not conceal my guilt.

6 I said, "I will confess my transgressions to God." *
   Then you forgave me the guilt of my sin.

7 Therefore all the faithful will make their prayers to you
         in time of trouble; *
   when the great waters overflow, they shall not reach them.

8 You are my hiding-place;
   you preserve me from trouble; *
   you surround me with shouts of deliverance.

9 "I will instruct you and teach you in the way that you
         should go; *
   I will guide you with my eye.

10 Do not be like horse or mule, which have
no understanding, *
who must be fitted with bit and bridle,
or else they will not stay near you."

11 Great are the tribulations of the wicked, *
but mercy embraces those who trust in the Most High.

12 Be glad, you righteous, and rejoice in God; *
shout for joy, all who are true of heart.

Psalm 33

1 Rejoice in God, you righteous; *
it is good for the just to sing praises.

2 Praise God with the harp; *
play upon the psaltery and lyre.

3 Sing for God a new song; *
sound a fanfare with all your skill upon the trumpet.

4 For your word, O God, is right, *
and all your works are sure.

5 You love righteousness and justice; *
your loving-kindness fills the whole earth.

6 By your word, O God, were the heavens made, *
by the breath of your mouth all the heavenly hosts.

7 You gather up the waters of the ocean as in a water-skin *
and store up the depths of the sea.

8 Let all the earth fear you; *
let all who dwell in the world stand in awe of you.

9 For you spoke, and it came to pass; *
      you commanded, and it stood fast.

10 You bring the will of the nations to naught *
      and thwart the designs of the peoples.

11 But your will stands fast for ever, *
      and the designs of your heart from age to age.

12 Happy is the nation that worships you, O Most High; *
      happy the people you have chosen to be your own!

13 You look down from heaven *
      and behold all the people in the world.

14 From where you sit enthroned you turn your gaze *
      on all who dwell on the earth.

15 You fashion all the hearts of them *
      and understand all their works.

16 There is no ruler that can be saved by a mighty army; *
      the strong are not delivered by their great strength.

17 The horse is a vain hope for deliverance; *
      for all its strength it cannot save.

18 But your eye, O God, is upon those who fear you, *
      on those who wait upon your love,

19 To pluck their lives from death *
      and to feed them in time of famine.

20 Our soul waits for you; *
      you are our help and our shield.

21 Indeed, our heart rejoices in you, *
     for in your holy Name we put our trust.

22 Let your loving-kindness, O God, be upon us, *
     as we have put our trust in you.

Psalm 34

1 I will bless God at all times, *
     and praise shall ever be in my mouth.

2 I will glory in the Most High; *
     let the humble hear and rejoice.

3 Proclaim with me the greatness of God; *
     let us exalt God's Name together.

4 I sought, and God answered me *
     and delivered me out of all my terror.

5 Look upon the Most High and be radiant, *
     and let not your faces be ashamed.

6 I called in my affliction, and God heard me *
     and saved me from all my troubles.

7 The angels encompass those who fear God, *
     and God will deliver them.

8 Taste and see that God is good; *
     happy are they who trust in the Most High!

9 Fear the Most High, you that are God's saints, *
     for those who fear God lack nothing.

10 The young lions lack and suffer hunger, *
     but those who seek God lack nothing that is good.

11 Come, children, and listen to me; *
    I will teach you the fear of God.

12 Who among you loves life *
    and desires long life to enjoy prosperity?

13 Keep your tongue from evil-speaking *
    and your lips from lying words.

14 Turn from evil and do good; *
    seek peace and pursue it.

15 The eyes of God are upon the righteous, *
    and the ears of God are open to their cry.

16 The face of God is against those who do evil, *
    to root out the remembrance of them from the earth.

17 The righteous cry, and God hears them *
    and delivers them from all their troubles.

18 God is near to the brokenhearted *
    and will save those whose spirits are crushed.

19 Many are the troubles of the righteous, *
    but God will deliver them out of them all.

20 God will keep safe all their bones; *
    not one of them shall be broken.

21 Evil shall slay the wicked, *
    and those who hate the righteous will be punished.

22 O God, you will ransom the life of your servants, *
    and none will be punished who trust in you.

Psalm 35

1 Fight those who fight me, O God; *
   attack those who are attacking me.

2 Take up shield and armor, *
   and rise up to help me.

3 Draw the sword and bar the way against those
           who pursue me; *
   say to my soul, "I am your salvation."

4 Let those who seek after my life be shamed and humbled; *
   let those who plot my ruin fall back and be dismayed.

5 Let them be like chaff before the wind, *
   and let the angel of God drive them away.

6 Let their way be dark and slippery, *
   and let the angel of God pursue them.

7 For they have secretly spread a net for me without a cause; *
   without a cause they have dug a pit to take me alive.

8 Let ruin come upon them unawares; *
   let them be caught in the net they hid;
   let them fall into the pit they dug.

9 Then I will be joyful in you, O Most High; *
   I will glory in your victory.

10 My very bones will say, "O God, who is like you? *
    You deliver the poor from those who are too strong
        for them,
    the poor and needy from those who rob them."

11 Malicious witnesses rise up against me; *
    they charge me with matters I know nothing about.

12 They pay me evil in exchange for good; *
    my soul is full of despair.

13 But when they were sick I dressed in sack-cloth *
    and humbled myself by fasting;

14 I prayed with my whole heart,
    as one would for a friend or a neighbor; *
        I behaved like those who mourn for their mothers,
        bowed down and grieving.

15 But when I stumbled, they were glad and gathered together;
    they gathered against me; *
        strangers whom I did not know tore me to pieces and
        would not stop.

16 They put me to the test and mocked me; *
    they gnashed at me with their teeth.

17 O God, how long will you look on? *
    Rescue me from the roaring beasts,
    and my life from the young lions.

18 I will give you thanks in the great congregation; *
    I will praise you in the mighty throng.

19 Do not let my treacherous foes rejoice over me, *
     nor let those who hate me without a cause
          wink at each other.

20 For they do not plan for peace, *
     but invent deceitful schemes against the quiet in the land.

21 They opened their mouths at me and said, *
     "Aha! we saw it with our own eyes."

22 You saw it, O God; do not be silent; *
     O God, be not far from me.

23 Awake, arise, to my cause; *
     to my defense, my God and my Savior!

24 Give me justice, O my God,
   according to your righteousness; *
     do not let them triumph over me.

25 Do not let them say in their hearts,
   "Aha! just what we want!" *
     Do not let them say, "We have swallowed you up."

26 Let all who rejoice at my ruin be ashamed and disgraced; *
     let those who boast against me be clothed with
          dismay and shame.

27 Let those who favor my cause sing out with joy and be glad; *
     let them say always, "Great are you, O God,
       you desire the prosperity of your servant."

28 And my tongue shall be talking of your righteousness *
     and of your praise all the day long.

Psalm 36

1 There is a voice of rebellion deep in the heart of the wicked; *
    there is no fear of God before their eyes.

2 They flatter themselves in their own eyes *
    that their hateful sin will not be found out.

3 The words of their mouths are wicked and deceitful; *
    they have left off acting wisely and doing good.

4 They think up wickedness upon their beds
  and have set themselves in no good way; *
    they do not abhor that which is evil.

5 Your love, O God, reaches to the heavens, *
    and your faithfulness to the clouds.

6 Your righteousness is like the strong mountains,
  your justice like the great deep; *
    you save all your creatures, O God.

7 How priceless is your love, O God; *
    your people take refuge under the shadow of your wings.

8 They feast upon the abundance of your house; *
    you give them drink from the river of your delights.

9 For with you is the well of life, *
    and in your light we see light.

10 Continue your loving-kindness to those who know you, *
    and your favor to those who are true of heart.

11 Let not the foot of the proud come near me, *
    nor the hand of the wicked push me aside.

12 See how they are fallen, those who work wickedness; *
    they are cast down and shall not be able to rise.

Seventh Day: Evening Prayer

PSALM 37

PART I

1 Do not fret yourself because of evildoers; *
    do not be jealous of those who do wrong.

2 For they shall soon wither like the grass, *
    and like the green grass fade away.

3 Put your trust in God and do good; *
    dwell in the land and feed on its riches.

4 Take delight in God, *
    who shall give you your heart's desire.

5 Commit your way to God and put your trust in God, *
    who will bring it to pass.

6 God will make your righteousness as clear as the light *
    and your just dealing as the noonday.

7 Be still before God; *
    for God wait patiently.

8 Do not fret yourself over the one who prospers, *
    the one who succeeds in evil schemes.

9 Refrain from anger, leave rage alone; *
    do not fret yourself, it leads only to evil.

10 For evildoers shall be cut off, *
    but those who wait upon God shall possess the land.

11 In a little while the wicked shall be no more; *
    you shall search out their place, but they will not be there.

12 But the lowly shall possess the land; *
    they will delight in abundance of peace.

13 The wicked plot against the righteous *
    and gnash at them with their teeth.

14 God laughs at the wicked, *
    seeing that their day will come.

15 The wicked draw their sword and bend their bow
    to strike down the poor and needy, *
    to slaughter those who are upright in their ways.

16 Their sword shall go through their own heart, *
    and their bow shall be broken.

17 The little that the righteous has *
    is better than great riches of the wicked.

18 For the power of the wicked shall be broken, *
    but God upholds the righteous.

PSALM 37: PART II

19 God cares for the lives of the faithful, *
    and their inheritance shall last for ever.

20 They shall not be ashamed in bad times, *
    and in days of famine they shall have enough.

21 As for the wicked, they shall perish, *
    and the enemies of God, like the glory of
        the meadows, shall vanish;
    they shall vanish like smoke.

22 The wicked borrow and do not repay, *
    but the righteous are generous in giving.

23 Those who are blest by God shall possess the land, *
    but those who are cursed shall be destroyed.

24 Our steps are directed by God, *
    who strengthens those whose ways are upright.

25 If they stumble, they shall not fall headlong, *
    for God holds them by the hand.

26 I have been young and now I am old, *
    but never have I seen the righteous forsaken
    or their children begging bread.

27 The righteous are always generous in their lending, *
    and their children shall be a blessing.

28 Turn from evil and do good, *
    and dwell in the land for ever.

29 For God loves justice *
    and does not forsake the faithful ones.

30 They shall be kept safe for ever, *
    but the offspring of the wicked shall be destroyed.

31 The righteous shall possess the land *
    and dwell in it for ever.

32 The mouth of the righteous utters wisdom, *
    and their tongue speaks what is right.

33 The law of their God is in their heart, *
    and their footsteps shall not falter.

34 The wicked spy on the righteous *
    and seek occasion to kill them.

35 But God will not abandon them to their hand, *
    nor let them be found guilty when brought to trial.

36 Wait upon God and keep God's way; *
    you will be raised up to possess the land,
    and when the wicked are cut off, you will see it.

37 I have seen the wicked in their arrogance, *
    flourishing like a tree in full leaf.

38 I went by, and behold, they were not there; *
    I searched for them, but they could not be found.

39 Mark those who are honest;
  observe the upright, *
    for there is a future for the peaceable.

40 Transgressors shall be destroyed, one and all; *
    the future of the wicked is cut off.

41 But the deliverance of the righteous comes from God, *
    who is their stronghold in time of trouble.

42 God will help them and rescue them; *
    the Holy One will rescue them from the wicked
        and deliver them,
    because they seek refuge in God.

PSALM 38

1 O God, do not rebuke me in your anger; *
   do not punish me in your wrath.

2 For your arrows have already pierced me, *
   and your hand presses hard upon me.

3 There is no health in my flesh
   because of your indignation; *
   there is no soundness in my body because of my sin.

4 For my iniquities overwhelm me; *
   like a heavy burden they are too much for me to bear.

5 My wounds stink and fester *
   by reason of my foolishness.

6 I am utterly bowed down and prostrate; *
   I go about in mourning all the day long.

7 My loins are filled with searing pain; *
   there is no health in my body.

8 I am utterly numb and crushed; *
   I wail, because of the groaning of my heart.

9 O God, you know all my desires, *
   and my sighing is not hidden from you.

10 My heart is pounding, my strength has failed me, *
   and the brightness of my eyes is gone from me.

11 My friends and companions draw back from my affliction; *
   my neighbors stand afar off.

12 Those who seek after my life lay snares for me; *
   those who strive to hurt me speak of my ruin
   and plot treachery all the day long.

13 But I am like the deaf who do not hear, *
   like those who are mute and do not open their mouth.

14 I have become like one who does not hear *
   and from whose mouth comes no defense.

15 For in you, O God, have I fixed my hope; *
   you will answer me, O my God.

16 For I said, "Do not let them rejoice at my expense, *
   those who gloat over me when my foot slips."

17 Truly, I am on the verge of falling, *
   and my pain is always with me.

18 I will confess my iniquity *
   and be sorry for my sin.

19 Those who are my enemies without cause are mighty, *
   and many in number are those who wrongfully hate me.

20 Those who repay evil for good slander me, *
   because I follow the course that is right.

21 O Holy One, do not forsake me; *
   be not far from me, O my God.

22 Make haste to help me, *
   O God of my salvation.

Psalm 39

1 I said, "I will keep watch upon my ways, *
    so that I do not offend with my tongue.

2 I will put a muzzle on my mouth *
    while the wicked are in my presence."

3 So I held my tongue and said nothing; *
    I refrained from rash words,
    but my pain became unbearable.

4 My heart was hot within me;
    while I pondered, the fire burst into flame; *
    I spoke out with my tongue:

5 O God, let me know my end and the number of my days, *
    so that I may know how short my life is.

6 You have given me a mere handful of days,
    and my lifetime is as nothing in your sight; *
    truly, even those who stand erect are but a puff of wind.

7 We walk about like a shadow,
    and in vain we are in turmoil; *
    we heap up riches and cannot tell who will gather them.

8 And now, what is my hope? *
    O God, my hope is in you.

9 Deliver me from all my transgressions, *
    and do not make me the taunt of the fool.

10 I fell silent and did not open my mouth, *
    for surely it was you that did it.

11 Take your affliction from me; *
     I am worn down by the blows of your hand.

12 With rebukes for sin you punish us;
     like a moth you eat away all that is dear to us; *
        truly, everyone is but a puff of wind.

13 Hear my prayer, O God,
     and give ear to my cry; *
        hold not your peace at my tears,

14 For I am but a sojourner with you, *
     a wayfarer, as all my forebears were.

15 Turn your gaze from me, that I may be glad again, *
     before I go my way and am no more.

Psalm 40

1 I waited patiently for you, O God; *
     you stooped to me and heard my cry.

2 You lifted me out of the desolate pit, out of the mire
        and clay; *
     you set my feet upon a high cliff and made
        my footing sure.

3 You put a new song in my mouth,
     a song of praise to our God; *
        many shall see, and stand in awe,
        and put their trust in you.

4 Happy are they who trust in you; *
     they do not resort to evil spirits or turn to false gods.

5 Great things are they that you have done, O God;
   how great your wonders and your plans for us; *
      there is none who can be compared with you.

6 Oh, that I could make them known and tell them, *
   but they are more than I can count.

7 In sacrifice and offering you take no pleasure *
   (you have given me ears to hear you);

8 Burnt-offering and sin-offering you have not required, *
   and so I said, "Behold, I come.

9 In the roll of the book it is written concerning me: *
   'I love to do your will, O my God;
   your law is deep in my heart.' "

10 I proclaimed righteousness in the great congregation; *
   behold, I did not restrain my lips,
   and that, O God, you know.

11 Your righteousness have I not hidden in my heart;
   I have spoken of your faithfulness and your deliverance; *
   I have not concealed your love and faithfulness from
      the great congregation.

12 You are the Holy One;
   do not withhold your compassion from me; *
   let your love and your faithfulness keep me safe for ever.

13 For innumerable troubles have crowded upon me;
   my sins have overtaken me, and I cannot see; *
   they are more in number than the hairs of my head,
   and my heart fails me.

14 Be pleased, O God, to deliver me; *
     O God, make haste to help me.

15 Let them be ashamed and altogether dismayed
     who seek after my life to destroy it; *
       let them draw back and be disgraced
       who take pleasure in my misfortune.

16 Let those who say "Aha!" and gloat over me be confounded
     because they are ashamed.

17 Let all who seek you rejoice in you and be glad; *
     let those who love your salvation continually say,
       "Great is the Holy One!"

18 Though I am poor and afflicted, *
     you will have regard for me.

19 You are my helper and my deliverer; *
     do not tarry, O my God.

Eighth Day: Evening Prayer

PSALM 41

1 Happy are they who consider the poor and needy! *
     God will deliver them in the time of trouble.

2 God preserves them and keeps them alive,
     so that they may be happy in the land, *
       and does not hand them over to the will of their enemies.

3 God sustains them on their sickbed *
     and ministers to them in their illness.

4 I said, "O God, be merciful to me; *
    heal me, for I have sinned against you."

5 My enemies are saying wicked things about me, *
    wondering when I will die and my name perish.

6 Even if they come to see me, they speak empty words; *
    their heart collects false rumors;
    they go outside and spread them.

7 All my enemies whisper together about me *
    and devise evil against me.

8 They say a deadly thing has fastened on me, *
    that I have taken to my bed and will never get up again.

9 Even my best friend, whom I trusted,
  who broke bread with me, *
    has spurned me and turned against me.

10 But you, O God, be merciful to me and raise me up, *
    and I shall repay them.

11 By this I know you are pleased with me, *
    that my enemy does not triumph over me.

12 In my integrity you hold me fast *
    and shall set me before your face for ever.

13 Blessed be the God of Israel, *
    from age to age. Amen. Amen.

BOOK TWO

PSALM 42

1 As the deer longs for the water-brooks, *
    so longs my soul for you, O God.

2 My soul is athirst for God, athirst for the living God; *
    when shall I come to appear before the presence of God?

3 My tears have been my food day and night, *
    while all day long they say to me,
    "Where now is your God?"

4 I pour out my soul when I think on these things: *
    how I went with the multitude and led them into the
        house of God,

5 With the voice of praise and thanksgiving, *
    among those who keep holy-day.

6 Why are you so full of heaviness, O my soul, *
    and why are you so disquieted within me?

7 Put your trust in God, *
    for I will yet give thanks to the Holy One,
    who is the help of my countenance, and my God.

8 My soul is heavy within me; *
    therefore I will remember you from the land of Jordan,
    and from the peak of Mizar among the heights of Hermon.

9 One deep calls to another in the noise of your cataracts; *
    all your rapids and floods have gone over me.

10 You grant me your loving-kindness in the daytime; *
    in the night season your song is with me,
    a prayer to the God of my life.

11 I will say to the God of my strength,
    "Why have you forgotten me, *
    and why do I go so heavily while the enemy oppresses me?"

12 While my bones are being broken, *
    my enemies mock me to my face;

13 All day long they mock me *
    and say to me, "Where now is your God?"

14 Why are you so full of heaviness, O my soul, *
    and why are you so disquieted within me?

15 Put your trust in God, *
    for I will yet give thanks to the Holy One,
    who is the help of my countenance, and my God.

PSALM 43

1 Give judgment for me, O God,
    and defend my cause against an ungodly people; *
    deliver me from the deceitful and the wicked.

2 For you are the God of my strength;
    why have you put me from you, *
    and why do I go so heavily while the enemy oppresses me?

3 Send out your light and your truth, that they may lead me, *
    and bring me to your holy hill
    and to your dwelling;

4 That I may go to the altar of God,
   to the God of my joy and gladness, *
      and on the harp I will give thanks to you, O God,
         my God.

5 Why are you so full of heaviness, O my soul, *
   and why are you so disquieted within me?

6 Put your trust in God, *
   for I will yet give thanks to the Holy One,
      who is the help of my countenance, and my God.

Ninth Day: Morning Prayer

PSALM 44

1 We have heard with our ears, O God,
   our forebears have told us, *
      the deeds you did in their days,
      in the days of old;

2 How with your hand you drove the peoples out
   and planted our forebears in the land; *
      how you destroyed nations and made your people flourish.

3 For they did not take the land by their sword,
   nor did their arm win the victory for them; *
      but your right hand, your arm, and the
         light of your countenance,
      because you favored them.

4 You are my Ruler and my God; *
   you command victories for Jacob.

5 Through you we pushed back our adversaries; *
    through your Name we trampled on those who
        rose up against us.

6 For I do not rely on my bow, *
    and my sword does not give me the victory.

7 Surely, you gave us victory over our adversaries *
    and put those who hate us to shame.

8 Every day we gloried in God, *
    and we will praise your Name for ever.

9 Nevertheless, you have rejected and humbled us *
    and do not go forth with our armies.

10 You have made us fall back before our adversary, *
    and our enemies have plundered us.

11 You have made us like sheep to be eaten *
    and have scattered us among the nations.

12 You are selling your people for a trifle *
    and are making no profit on the sale of them.

13 You have made us the scorn of our neighbors, *
    a mockery and derision to those around us.

14 You have made us a byword among the nations, *
    a laughing-stock among the peoples.

15 My humiliation is daily before me, *
    and shame has covered my face,

16 Because of the taunts of the mockers and blasphemers, *
    because of the enemy and avenger.

17 All this has come upon us; *
       yet we have not forgotten you,
       nor have we betrayed your covenant.

18 Our heart never turned back, *
       nor did our footsteps stray from your path,

19 Though you thrust us down into a place of misery *
       and covered us over with deep darkness.

20 If we have forgotten the Name of our God *
       or stretched out our hands to some strange god,

21 Will God not find it out, *
       for God knows the secrets of the heart.

22 Indeed, for your sake we are killed all the day long; *
       we are accounted as sheep for the slaughter.

23 Awake, O God! Why are you sleeping? *
       Arise; do not reject us for ever.

24 Why have you hidden your face *
       and forgotten our affliction and oppression?

25 We sink down into the dust; *
       our body cleaves to the ground.

26 Rise up, and help us, *
       and save us, for the sake of your steadfast love.

Psalm 45

1 My heart is stirring with a noble song;
       let me recite what I have fashioned for the king; *
       my tongue shall be the pen of a skilled writer.

2 You are the fairest of men; *
    grace flows from your lips,
    because God has blessed you for ever.

3 Strap your sword upon your thigh, O mighty warrior, *
    in your pride and in your majesty.

4 Ride out and conquer in the cause of truth *
    and for the sake of justice.

5 Your right hand will show you marvelous things; *
    your arrows are very sharp, O mighty warrior.

6 The peoples are falling at your feet, *
    and the king's enemies are losing heart.

7 Your throne, O God, endures for ever and ever; *
    a scepter of righteousness is the scepter of your realm;
    you love righteousness and hate iniquity.

8 Therefore God, your God, has anointed you *
    with the oil of gladness above your companions.

9 All your garments are fragrant with myrrh, aloes and cassia, *
    and the music of strings from ivory palaces makes you glad.

10 The royal daughters stand among the ladies of the court; *
    on your right hand is the queen,
    adorned with the gold of Ophir.

11 "Hear, O daughter, consider and listen closely; *
    forget your people and your parents' house.

12 The king will have pleasure in your beauty; *
    you are committed to him; therefore do him honor.

13 The people of Tyre are here with a gift; *
    the rich among the people seek your favor."

14 All glorious is the princess as she enters; *
    her gown is cloth-of-gold.

15 In embroidered apparel she is brought to the king; *
    after her the bridesmaids follow in procession.

16 With joy and gladness they are brought *
    and enter into the palace of the king.

17 "In place of fathers, O king, you shall have sons; *
    you shall make them princes over all the earth.

18 I will make your name to be remembered
from one generation to another; *
    therefore nations will praise you for ever and ever."

PSALM 46

1 God is our refuge and strength, *
    a very present help in trouble.

2 Therefore we will not fear, though the earth be moved, *
    and though the mountains be toppled into the depths
        of the sea;

3 Though its waters rage and foam, *
    and though the mountains tremble at its tumult.

4 The God of hosts is with us; *
    the God of Jacob is our stronghold.

5 There is a river whose streams make glad the city of God, *
    the holy habitation of the Most High.

6 God is in the midst of the city;
 it shall not be overthrown; *
  God shall help it at the break of day.

7 The nations make much ado, and the realms are shaken; *
  God has spoken, and the earth shall melt away.

8 The God of hosts is with us; *
  the God of Jacob is our stronghold.

9 Come now and look upon the works of the Most High, *
  who does awesome things on earth.

10 It is God who makes war to cease in all the world, *
  who breaks the bow and shatters the spear,
  and burns the shields with fire.

11 "Be still, then, and know that I am God; *
  I will be exalted among the nations;
  I will be exalted in the earth."

12 The God of hosts is with us; *
  the God of Jacob is our stronghold.

Ninth Day: Evening Prayer

PSALM 47

1 Clap your hands, all you peoples; *
  shout to God with a cry of joy.

2 For God Most High is to be feared; *
  God is the great Sovereign over all the earth.

3 God subdues the peoples under us *
  and the nations under our feet.

4 God chooses our inheritance for us, *
   the pride of Jacob whom God loves.

5 God has gone up with a shout, *
   the Most High with the sound of the ram's-horn.

6 Sing praises to God, sing praises; *
   sing praises to our Sovereign, sing praises.

7 For God is Sovereign over all the earth; *
   sing praises with all your skill.

8 God reigns over the nations; *
   God sits upon the holy throne.

9 The nobles of the peoples have gathered together *
   with the people of the God of Abraham.

10 The rulers of the earth belong to God, *
   who is highly exalted.

PSALM 48

1 God is great and highly to be praised; *
   in the city of our God is the holy hill.

2 Beautiful and lofty, the joy of all the earth, is the hill of Zion, *
   the very center of the world and the city
      of the great Sovereign.

3 God is in its citadels; *
   God is known to be its sure refuge.

4 Behold, the monarchs of the earth assembled *
   and marched forward together.

5 They looked and were astounded; *
   they retreated and fled in terror.

6 Trembling seized them there; *
   they writhed like a woman in childbirth,
   like ships of the sea when the east wind shatters them.

7 As we have heard, so have we seen,
   in the city of the God of hosts, in the city of our God; *
   God has established it for ever.

8 We have waited in silence on your loving-kindness, O God, *
   in the midst of your temple.

9 Your praise, like your Name, O God, reaches to
            the world's end; *
   your right hand is full of justice.

10 Let Mount Zion be glad
   and the cities of Judah rejoice, *
   because of your judgments.

11 Make the circuit of Zion;
   walk round about it; *
   count the number of its towers.

12 Consider well its bulwarks;
   examine its strongholds, *
   that you may tell those who come after:

13 This God is our God for ever and ever *
   and shall be our guide for evermore.

Psalm 49

1 Hear this, all you peoples;
   hearken, all you who dwell in the world, *
      you of high degree and low, rich and poor together.

2 My mouth shall speak of wisdom, *
   and my heart shall meditate on understanding.

3 I will incline my ear to a proverb *
   and set forth my riddle upon the harp.

4 Why should I be afraid in evil days, *
   when the wickedness of those at my heels surrounds me,

5 The wickedness of those who put their trust in their goods, *
   and boast of their great riches?

6 We can never ransom ourselves, *
   or deliver to God the price of our life;

7 For the ransom of our life is so great, *
   that we should never have enough to pay it,

8 In order to live for ever and ever, *
   and never see the grave.

9 For we see that the wise die also;
   like the dull and stupid they perish *
      and leave their wealth to those who come after them.

10 Their graves shall be their homes for ever,
    their dwelling places from generation to generation, *
       though they call the lands after their own names.

11 Even though honored, they cannot live for ever; *
    they are like the beasts that perish.

12 Such is the way of those who foolishly trust in themselves, *
    and the end of those who delight in their own words.

13 Like a flock of sheep they are destined to die;
   Death is their shepherd; *
    they go down straightway to the grave.

14 Their form shall waste away, *
    and the land of the dead shall be their home.

15 But God will ransom my life *
    and will snatch me from the grasp of death.

16 Do not be envious when some become rich *
    or when the grandeur of their house increases,

17 For they will carry nothing away at their death, *
    nor will their grandeur follow them.

18 Though they thought highly of themselves while they lived *
    and were praised for their success,

19 They shall join the company of their forebears, *
    who will never see the light again.

20 Those who are honored, but have no understanding, *
    are like the beasts that perish.

Tenth Day: Morning Prayer

PSALM 50

1 The God of gods has spoken; *
   God has called the earth from the rising of the sun to
     its setting.

2 Out of Zion, perfect in its beauty, *
    God is revealed in glory.

3 O God, you will come and will not keep silence; *
    before you there is a consuming flame,
    and round about you a raging storm.

4 You call the heavens and the earth from above *
    to witness the judgment of your people.

5 "Gather before me my loyal followers, *
    those who have made a covenant with me
    and sealed it with sacrifice."

6 Let the heavens declare the rightness of your cause, *
    for you alone are judge.

7 "Hear, O my people, and I will speak:
    O Israel, I will bear witness against you, *
    for I am God, your God.

8 I do not accuse you because of your sacrifices; *
    your offerings are always before me.

9 I will take no bull-calf from your stalls *
    nor he-goats out of your pens;

10 For all the beasts of the forest are mine, *
    the herds in their thousands upon the hills.

11 I know every bird in the sky, *
    and the creatures of the fields are in my sight.

12 If I were hungry, I would not tell you, *
    for the whole world is mine and all that is in it.

13 Do you think I eat the flesh of bulls *
    or drink the blood of goats?

14 Offer to God a sacrifice of thanksgiving, *
    and make good your vows to the Most High.

15 Call upon me in the day of trouble; *
    I will deliver you, and you shall honor me."

16 But to the wicked God says: *
    "Why do you recite my statutes
    and take my covenant upon your lips,

17 Since you refuse discipline *
    and toss my words behind your back?

18 When you see thieves, you make them your friends, *
    and you cast in your lot with adulterers.

19 You have loosed your lips for evil *
    and harnessed your tongue to a lie.

20 You are always speaking evil of your family *
    and slandering your own mother's child.

21 These things you have done, and I kept still, *
    and you thought that I am like you."

22 "I have made my accusation; *
    I have put my case in order before your eyes.

23 Consider this well, you who forget God, *
    lest I rend you and there be none to deliver you.

24 Whoever offers me the sacrifice of thanksgiving honors me; *
    but to those who keep in my way will I show
        the salvation of God."

Psalm 51

1 Have mercy on me, O God, according to
       your loving-kindness; *
    in your great compassion blot out my offenses.

2 Wash me through and through from my wickedness, *
    and cleanse me from my sin.

3 For I know my transgressions, *
    and my sin is ever before me.

4 Against you only have I sinned *
    and done what is evil in your sight.

5 And so you are justified when you speak *
    and upright in your judgment.

6 Indeed, I have been wicked from my birth, *
    a sinner from my mother's womb.

7 For behold, you look for truth deep within me *
    and will make me understand wisdom secretly.

8 Purge me from my sin, and I shall be pure; *
    wash me, and I shall be clean indeed.

9 Make me hear of joy and gladness, *
    that the body you have broken may rejoice.

10 Hide your face from my sins, *
     and blot out all my iniquities.

11 Create in me a clean heart, O God, *
     and renew a right spirit within me.

12 Cast me not away from your presence, *
     and take not your holy Spirit from me.

13 Give me the joy of your saving help again, *
   and sustain me with your bountiful Spirit.

14 I shall teach your ways to the wicked, *
   and sinners shall return to you.

15 Deliver me from death, O God, *
   and my tongue shall sing of your righteousness,
   O God of my salvation.

16 Open my lips, O God, *
   and my mouth shall proclaim your praise.

17 Had you desired it, I would have offered sacrifice, *
   but you take no delight in burnt-offerings.

18 The sacrifice of God is a troubled spirit; *
   a broken and contrite heart, O God, you will not despise.

19 Be favorable and gracious to Zion, *
   and rebuild the walls of Jerusalem.

20 Then you will be pleased with the appointed sacrifices,
   with burnt-offerings and oblations; *
   then shall they offer young bullocks upon your altar.

PSALM 52

1 You tyrant, why do you boast of wickedness *
   against the godly all day long?

2 You plot ruin;
   your tongue is like a sharpened razor, *
   O worker of deception.

3 You love evil more than good *
   and lying more than speaking the truth.

4 You love all words that hurt, *
   O you deceitful tongue.

5 Oh, that God would demolish you utterly, *
   topple you, and snatch you from your dwelling,
   and root you out of the land of the living!

6 The righteous shall see and tremble, *
   and they shall laugh at the tyrant, saying,

7 "This is the one who did not take God for a refuge, *
   but trusted in great wealth
   and relied upon wickedness."

8 But I am like a green olive tree in the house of God; *
   I trust in the mercy of God for ever and ever.

9 I will give you thanks for what you have done *
   and declare the goodness of your Name
      in the presence of the godly.

Tenth Day: Evening Prayer

Psalm 53

1 The foolish say in their hearts, "There is no God." *
   All are corrupt and commit abominable acts;
   there is none who does any good.

2 God looks down from heaven upon us all, *
   to see if there is any who is wise,
   if there is one who seeks after God.

3 Every one has proved faithless;
   all alike have turned bad; *
      there is none who does good; no, not one.

4 Have they no knowledge, those evildoers *
      who eat up my people like bread
      and do not call upon God?

5 See how greatly they tremble,
   such trembling as never was, *
      for God has scattered the bones of the enemy;
      they are put to shame, because God has rejected them.

6 Oh, that Israel's deliverance would come out of Zion! *
      When God restores the fortunes of the people,
      Jacob will rejoice and Israel be glad.

PSALM 54

1 Save me, O God, by your Name; *
      in your might, defend my cause.

2 Hear my prayer, O God; *
      give ear to the words of my mouth.

3 For the arrogant have risen up against me,
   and the ruthless have sought my life, *
      those who have no regard for God.

4 Behold, God is my helper; *
      it is God who sustains my life.

5 Render evil to those who spy on me; *
      in your faithfulness, destroy them.

6 I will offer you a freewill sacrifice *
    and praise your Name, O God, for it is good.

7 For you have rescued me from every trouble, *
    and my eye has seen the ruin of my foes.

Psalm 55

1 Hear my prayer, O God; *
    do not hide yourself from my petition.

2 Listen to me and answer me; *
    I have no peace, because of my cares.

3 I am shaken by the noise of the enemy *
    and by the pressure of the wicked;

4 For they have cast an evil spell upon me *
    and are set against me in fury.

5 My heart quakes within me, *
    and the terrors of death have fallen upon me.

6 Fear and trembling have come over me, *
    and horror overwhelms me.

7 And I said, "Oh, that I had wings like a dove! *
    I would fly away and be at rest.

8 I would flee to a far-off place *
    and make my lodging in the wilderness.

9 I would hasten to escape *
    from the stormy wind and tempest."

10 Swallow them up, O God; confound their speech, *
    for I have seen violence and strife in the city.

11 Day and night the sentries make their rounds upon its walls, *
  but trouble and misery are in the midst of it.

12 There is corruption at its heart; *
  its streets are never free of oppression and deceit.

13 For had it been an adversary who taunted me,
  then I could have borne it; *
    or had it been enemies who vaunted themselves against me,
    then I could have hidden from them.

14 But it was you, someone after my own heart, *
  my companion, my own familiar friend.

15 We took sweet counsel together *
  and walked with the throng in the house of God.

16 Let death come upon them suddenly;
  let them go down alive into the grave, *
    for wickedness is in their dwellings, in their very midst.

17 But I will call upon God, *
  and God will deliver me.

18 In the evening, in the morning, and at noonday,
  I will complain and lament, *
    and God will hear my voice.

19 God will bring me safely back from the battle
      waged against me, *
  for there are many who fight me.

20 God, who is enthroned of old, will hear me and
      bring them down; *
  they never change; they do not fear God.

PSALM 55   83

21 My companions have stretched forth their hands
        against their comrade; *
    they have broken their covenant.

22 Their speech is softer than butter, *
    but war is in their hearts.

23 Their words are smoother than oil, *
    but they are drawn swords.

24 Cast your burden upon God
    who will sustain you; *
        God will never let the righteous stumble.

25 For you will bring the bloodthirsty and deceitful *
    down to the pit of destruction, O God.

26 They shall not live out half their days, *
    but I will put my trust in you.

Eleventh Day: Morning Prayer

Psalm 56

1 Have mercy on me, O God,
    for my enemies are hounding me; *
        all day long they assault and oppress me.

2 They hound me all the day long; *
    truly there are many who fight against me, O Most High.

3 Whenever I am afraid, *
    I will put my trust in you.

4 In God, whose word I praise,
  in God I trust and will not be afraid, *
    for what can flesh do to me?

5 All day long they damage my cause; *
    their only thought is to do me evil.

6 They band together; they lie in wait; *
    they spy upon my footsteps,
    because they seek my life.

7 Shall they escape despite their wickedness? *
    O God, in your anger, cast down the peoples.

8 You have noted my lamentation;
  put my tears into your bottle; *
    are they not recorded in your book?

9 Whenever I call upon you, my enemies will be put to flight; *
    this I know, for God is on my side.

10 In God, whose word I praise,
   in God I trust and will not be afraid, *
     for what can mortals do to me?

11 I am bound by the vow I made to you, O God; *
     I will present to you thank-offerings;

12 For you have rescued my soul from death and
              my feet from stumbling, *
     that I may walk before you in the light of the living.

Psalm 57

1 Be merciful to me, O God, be merciful,
  for I have taken refuge in you; *
    in the shadow of your wings will I take refuge
    until this time of trouble has gone by.

2 I will call upon you, O Most High God, *
    you who maintain my cause.

3 You will send from heaven and save me;
  you will confound those who trample upon me; *
    you will send forth your love and your faithfulness.

4 I lie in the midst of lions that devour the people; *
    their teeth are spears and arrows,
    their tongue a sharp sword.

5 They have laid a net for my feet,
  and I am bowed low; *
    they have dug a pit before me,
    but have fallen into it themselves.

6 Exalt yourself above the heavens, O God, *
    and your glory over all the earth.

7 My heart is firmly fixed, O God, my heart is fixed; *
    I will sing and make melody.

8 Wake up, my spirit;
  awake, lute and harp; *
    I myself will waken the dawn.

9 I will confess you among the peoples, O God; *
    I will sing praise to you among the nations.

10 For your loving-kindness is greater than the heavens, *
 and your faithfulness reaches to the clouds.

11 Exalt yourself above the heavens, O God, *
 and your glory over all the earth.

PSALM 58

1 Do you indeed decree righteousness, you rulers; *
 do you judge the peoples with equity?

2 No; you devise evil in your hearts, *
 and your hands deal out violence in the land.

3 The wicked are perverse from the womb; *
 liars go astray from their birth.

4 They are as venomous as a serpent; *
 they are like the deaf adder which stops its ears,

5 Which does not heed the voice of the charmer, *
 no matter how skillful the charming.

6 O God, break their teeth in their mouths; *
 pull the fangs of the young lions, O God.

7 Let them vanish like water that runs off; *
 let them wither like trodden grass.

8 Let them be like the snail that melts away, *
 like a stillborn child that never sees the sun.

9 Before they bear fruit, let them be cut down like a brier; *
 like thorns and thistles let them be swept away.

10 The righteous will be glad when they see the vengeance; *
 they will bathe their feet in the blood of the wicked.

11 And they will say,
  "Surely, there is a reward for the righteous; *
    surely, there is a God who rules in the earth."

Eleventh Day: Evening Prayer

PSALM 59

1 Rescue me from my enemies, O God; *
    protect me from those who rise up against me.

2 Rescue me from evildoers, *
    and save me from those who thirst for my blood.

3 See how they lie in wait for my life,
  how the mighty gather together against me; *
    not for any offense or fault of mine, O God.

4 Not because of any guilt of mine, *
    they run and prepare themselves for battle.

5 Rouse yourself, come to my side and see, *
    for you, O God of hosts, are Israel's God.

6 Awake, and punish all the ungodly; *
    show no mercy to those who are faithless and evil.

7 They go to and fro in the evening; *
    they snarl like dogs and run about the city.

8 Behold, they boast with their mouths,
  and taunts are on their lips; *
    "For who," they say, "will hear us?"

9 But you, O God, you laugh at them; *
　　you laugh all the ungodly to scorn.

10 My eyes are fixed on you, O my Strength; *
　　for you, O God, are my stronghold.

11 My merciful God comes to meet me; *
　　God will let me look in triumph on my enemies.

12 Slay them, O God, lest my people forget; *
　　send them reeling by your might,
　　and put them down, O God our shield.

13 For the sins of their mouths, for the words of their lips,
　　for the cursing and lies that they utter, *
　　let them be caught in their pride.

14 Make an end of them in your wrath; *
　　make an end of them, and they shall be no more.

15 Let everyone know that God rules in Jacob *
　　and to the ends of the earth.

16 They go to and fro in the evening; *
　　they snarl like dogs and run about the city.

17 They forage for food, *
　　and if they are not filled, they howl.

18 For my part, I will sing of your strength; *
　　I will celebrate your love in the morning;

19 For you have become my stronghold, *
　　a refuge in the day of my trouble.

20 To you, O my Strength, will I sing; *
    for you, O God, are my stronghold and my merciful God.

PSALM 60

1 O God, you have cast us off and broken us; *
    you have been angry;
    oh, take us back to you again.

2 You have shaken the earth and split it open; *
    repair the cracks in it, for it totters.

3 You have made your people know hardship; *
    you have given us wine that makes us stagger.

4 You have set up a banner for those who fear you, *
    to be a refuge from the power of the bow.

5 Save us by your right hand and answer us, *
    that those who are dear to you may be delivered.

6 God spoke from the holy place and said: *
    "I will exult and parcel out Shechem;
    I will divide the valley of Succoth.

7 Gilead is mine and Manasseh is mine; *
    Ephraim is my helmet and Judah my scepter.

8 Moab is my wash-basin;
    on Edom I throw down my sandal to claim it, *
    and over Philistia will I shout in triumph."

9 Who will lead me into the strong city; *
    who will bring me into Edom?

10 Have you not cast us off, O God? *
    You no longer go out, O God, with our armies.

11 Grant us your help against the enemy, *
    for all human help is in vain.

12 With you, O God, we will do valiant deeds, *
    and you will tread our enemies under foot.

PSALM 61

1 Hear my cry, O God, *
    and listen to my prayer.

2 I call upon you from the ends of the earth
  with heaviness in my heart; *
    set me upon the rock that is higher than I.

3 For you have been my refuge, *
    a strong tower against the enemy.

4 I will dwell in your house for ever; *
    I will take refuge under the cover of your wings.

5 For you, O God, have heard my vows; *
    you have granted me the heritage of those who
        fear your Name.

6 Add length of days to the king's life; *
    let his years extend over many generations.

7 Let him sit enthroned before God for ever; *
    bid love and faithfulness watch over him.

8 So will I always sing the praise of your Name, *
    and day by day I will fulfill my vows.

PSALM 62

1 For God alone my soul in silence waits; *
   from God comes my salvation.

2 God alone is my rock and my salvation, *
   my stronghold, so that I shall not be greatly shaken.

3 How long will you assail me to crush me,
   all of you together, *
     as if you were a leaning fence, a toppling wall?

4 They seek only to bring me down from my place of honor; *
   lies are their chief delight.

5 They bless with their lips, *
   but in their hearts they curse.

6 For God alone my soul in silence waits; *
   truly, there is my hope.

7 God alone is my rock and my salvation, *
   my stronghold, so that I shall not be shaken.

8 In God is my safety and my honor; *
   God is my strong rock and my refuge.

9 Put your trust in God always, O people; *
   pour out your hearts before the One who is our refuge.

10 Those of high degree are but a fleeting breath; *
    even those of low estate cannot be trusted.

11 On the scales they are lighter than a breath, *
    all of them together.

12 Put no trust in extortion;
    in robbery take no empty pride; *
       though wealth increase, set not your heart upon it.

13 God has spoken once, twice have I heard it, *
    that power belongs to God.

14 Steadfast love is yours, O God, *
    for you repay everyone according to their deeds.

PSALM 63

1 O God, you are my God; eagerly I seek you; *
    my soul thirsts for you, my flesh faints for you,
    as in a barren and dry land where there is no water.

2 Therefore I have gazed upon you in your holy place, *
    that I might behold your power and your glory.

3 For your loving-kindness is better than life itself; *
    my lips shall give you praise.

4 So will I bless you as long as I live *
    and lift up my hands in your Name.

5 My soul is content, as with marrow and fatness, *
    and my mouth praises you with joyful lips,

6 When I remember you upon my bed *
    and meditate on you in the night watches.

7 For you have been my helper, *
    and under the shadow of your wings I will rejoice.

8 My soul clings to you; *
    your right hand holds me fast.

9 May those who seek my life to destroy it *
    go down into the depths of the earth;

10 Let them fall upon the edge of the sword, *
    and let them be food for jackals.

11 But the sovereign will rejoice in God;
    all those who swear by God will be glad, *
    for the mouth of those who speak lies shall be stopped.

PSALM 64

1 Hear my voice, O God, when I complain; *
    protect my life from fear of the enemy.

2 Hide me from the conspiracy of the wicked, *
    from the mob of evildoers.

3 They sharpen their tongue like a sword *
    and aim their bitter words like arrows,

4 That they may shoot down the blameless from ambush; *
    they shoot without warning and are not afraid.

5 They hold fast to their evil course; *
    they plan how they may hide their snares.

6 They say, "Who will see us;
    who will find out our crimes? *
    We have thought out a perfect plot."

7 The human mind and heart are a mystery, *
    but God will loose an arrow at them,
    and suddenly they will be wounded.

8 God will make them trip over their tongues, *
   and all who see them will shake their heads.

9 Everyone will stand in awe and declare God's deeds; *
   they will recognize the works of the Most High.

10 The righteous will rejoice and put their trust in God, *
   and all who are true of heart will glory.

Twelfth Day: Evening Prayer

PSALM 65

1 You are to be praised, O God, in Zion; *
   to you shall vows be performed in Jerusalem.

2 To you that hear prayer shall all flesh come, *
   because of their transgressions.

3 Our sins are stronger than we are, *
   but you will blot them out.

4 Happy are they whom you choose
   and draw to your courts to dwell there; *
      they will be satisfied by the beauty of your house,
      by the holiness of your temple.

5 Awesome things will you show us in your righteousness,
   O God of our salvation, *
      O Hope of all the ends of the earth
      and of the seas that are far away.

6 You make fast the mountains by your power; *
   they are girded about with might.

7 You still the roaring of the seas, *
　　the roaring of their waves,
　　and the clamor of the peoples.

8 Those who dwell at the ends of the earth will tremble
　　　　at your marvelous signs; *
　　you make the dawn and the dusk to sing for joy.

9 You visit the earth and water it abundantly;
　　you make it very plenteous; *
　　the river of God is full of water.

10 You prepare the grain, *
　　for so you provide for the earth.

11 You drench the furrows and smooth out the ridges; *
　　with heavy rain you soften the ground and bless its increase.

12 You crown the year with your goodness, *
　　and your paths overflow with plenty.

13 May the fields of the wilderness be rich for grazing *
　　and the hills be clothed with joy.

14 May the meadows cover themselves with flocks
　　and the valleys cloak themselves with grain; *
　　let them shout for joy and sing.

PSALM 66

1 Be joyful in God, all you lands; *
　　sing the glory of God's Name;
　　sing the glory of God's praise.

2 Say to God, "How awesome are your deeds; *
    because of your great strength your enemies
       cringe before you.

3 All the earth bows down before you, *
    sings to you, sings out your Name."

4 Come now and see the works of God, *
    how wonderful are these doings toward all people.

5 God turned the sea into dry land,
    so that they went through the water on foot, *
       and there we rejoiced in God,

6 Whose might rules for ever,
    whose eyes keep watch over the nations; *
       let not the rebellious lift up their heads.

7 Bless our God, you peoples; *
    let the sound of praise be heard;

8 God holds our souls in life *
    and will not allow our feet to slip.

9 For you, O God, have proved us; *
    you have tried us just as silver is tried.

10 You brought us into the snare *
    and laid heavy burdens upon our backs.

11 You let enemies ride over our heads;
    we went through fire and water, *
       but you brought us out into a place of refreshment.

12 I will enter your house with burnt-offerings
   and will pay you my vows, *
      which I promised with my lips
      and spoke with my mouth when I was in trouble.

13 I will offer you sacrifices of fat beasts
   with the smoke of rams; *
      I will give you oxen and goats.

14 Come and listen, all you who fear God, *
      and I will tell you what God has done for me.

15 I called out to God with my mouth, *
      and high praise was on my tongue.

16 If I had found evil in my heart, *
      God would not have heard me,

17 But in truth God has heard me *
      and has attended to the voice of my prayer.

18 Blessed be God, who has not rejected my prayer, *
      nor withheld steadfast love from me.

PSALM 67

1 Be merciful to us, O God, and bless us; *
      show us the light of your countenance and come to us.

2 Let your ways be known upon earth, *
      your saving health among all nations.

3 Let the peoples praise you, O God; *
      let all the peoples praise you.

4 Let the nations be glad and sing for joy, *
    for you judge the peoples with equity
    and guide all the nations upon earth.

5 Let the peoples praise you, O God; *
    let all the peoples praise you.

6 The earth has brought forth its increase; *
    may you, our own God, give us your blessing.

7 May you give us your blessing, *
    and may all the ends of the earth stand in awe of you.

Thirteenth Day: Morning Prayer

PSALM 68

1 Arise, O God, and let your enemies be scattered; *
    let those who hate you flee before you.

2 Let them vanish like smoke when the wind drives it away; *
    as the wax melts at the fire, so let the wicked perish at
        your presence, O God.

3 But let the righteous be glad and rejoice before you; *
    let them also be merry and joyful.

4 We sing praises to your holy Name;
    we exalt the One who rides upon the heavens; *
    yours is the Name in which we rejoice!

5 Guardian of orphans, defender of widows, *
    God, in your holy habitation!

6 You give the solitary a home and bring forth prisoners
        into freedom, *
   but the rebels shall live in dry places.

7 O God, when you went forth before your people, *
   when you marched through the wilderness,

8 The earth shook, and the skies poured down rain
  at the presence of God, the God of Sinai, *
   at the presence of God, the God of Israel.

9 You sent a gracious rain, O God, upon your inheritance; *
   you refreshed the land when it was weary.

10 Your people found their home in it; *
   in your goodness, O God, you have made provision
       for the poor.

11 You gave the word; *
   great was the company of those who bore the tidings:

12 "Rulers with their armies are fleeing away; *
   the ones at home are dividing the spoils."

13 Though you lingered among the sheepfolds, *
   you shall be like a dove whose wings
      are covered with silver,
   whose feathers are like green gold.

14 When the Almighty scattered rulers, *
   it was like snow falling in Zalmon.

15 O mighty mountain, O hill of Bashan! *
   O rugged mountain, O hill of Bashan!

16 Why do you look with envy, O rugged mountain,
   at the hill which God chose for a resting place? *
       Truly, God will dwell there for ever.

17 Your chariots, O God, are twenty thousand,
   even thousands of thousands; *
       you come in holiness from Sinai.

18 You have gone up on high and led captivity captive;
   you have received gifts even from your enemies, *
       that the Holy One might dwell among them.

19 Blest are you, O God, day by day, *
       the God of our salvation, who bears our burdens.

20 You are our God, the God of our salvation; *
       you are the one by whom we escape death.

21 You will crush the heads of your enemies *
       and the hairy scalp of those who go on still
           in their wickedness.

22 You have said, "I will bring my people back from Bashan; *
       I will bring them back from the depths of the sea;

23 That their feet may be dipped in blood, *
       the tongues of their dogs in the blood of their enemies."

24 They see your procession, O God, *
       your procession into the sanctuary, my God and
           my Sovereign.

25 The singers go before, musicians follow after, *
       in the midst of maidens playing upon the hand-drums.

26 Bless God in the congregation; *
   bless God, you that are of the fountain of Israel.

27 There is Benjamin, least of the tribes, at the head;
   the rulers of Judah in a company, *
      and the rulers of Zebulon and Naphtali.

28 Send forth your strength, O God; *
   establish, O God, what you have wrought for us.

29 Rulers shall bring gifts to you, *
   for your temple's sake at Jerusalem.

30 Rebuke the wild beast of the reeds, *
   and the peoples, a herd of wild bulls with its calves.

31 Trample down those who lust after silver; *
   scatter the peoples that delight in war.

32 Let tribute be brought out of Egypt; *
   let Ethiopia stretch out its hands to you.

33 Sing to God, O nations of the earth; *
   sing praises to the Holy One,

34 Who rides in the heavens, the ancient heavens, *
   who sends forth a voice, a mighty voice.

35 Ascribe power to God, *
   whose majesty is over Israel,
   whose strength is in the skies.

36 How wonderful is God in the holy places; *
   the God of Israel giving strength and power to the people;
   blessed be God!

PSALM 69

1 Save me, O God, *
   for the waters have risen up to my neck.

2 I am sinking in deep mire, *
   and there is no firm ground for my feet.

3 I have come into deep waters, *
   and the torrent washes over me.

4 I have grown weary with my crying;
  my throat is inflamed; *
   my eyes have failed from looking for my God.

5 Those who hate me without a cause are more than
       the hairs of my head;
  my lying foes who would destroy me are mighty. *
   Must I then give back what I never stole?

6 O God, you know my foolishness, *
   and my faults are not hidden from you.

7 Let not those who hope in you be put to shame through me,
   O God of hosts; *
   let not those who seek you be disgraced because of me,
     O God of Israel.

8 Surely for your sake have I suffered reproach, *
   and shame has covered my face.

9 I have become a stranger to my own kindred, *
   an outcast to my mother's children.

PSALM 69   103

10 Zeal for your house has eaten me up; *
    the scorn of those who scorn you has fallen upon me.

11 I humbled myself with fasting, *
    but that was turned to my reproach.

12 I put on sack-cloth also *
    and became a byword among them.

13 Those who sit at the gate murmur against me, *
    and the drunkards make songs about me.

14 But as for me, this is my prayer to you *
    at the time you have set, O God.

15 "In your great mercy, O God, *
    answer me with your unfailing help.

16 Save me from the mire; do not let me sink; *
    let me be rescued from those who hate me
    and out of the deep waters.

17 Let not the torrent of waters wash over me,
neither let the deep swallow me up; *
    do not let the Pit shut its mouth upon me.

18 Answer me, O God, for your love is kind; *
    in your great compassion, turn to me."

19 "Hide not your face from your servant; *
    be swift and answer me, for I am in distress.

20 Draw near to me and redeem me; *
    because of my enemies deliver me.

21 You know my reproach, my shame, and my dishonor; *
    my adversaries are all in your sight."

22 Reproach has broken my heart, and it cannot be healed; *
   I looked for sympathy, but there was none,
   for comforters, but I could find no one.

23 They gave me gall to eat, *
   and when I was thirsty, they gave me vinegar to drink.

24 Let the table before them be a trap *
   and their sacred feasts a snare.

25 Let their eyes be darkened, that they may not see, *
   and give them continual trembling in their loins.

26 Pour out your indignation upon them, *
   and let the fierceness of your anger overtake them.

27 Let their camp be desolate, *
   and let there be none to dwell in their tents.

28 For they persecute the one whom you have stricken *
   and add to the pain of those whom you have pierced.

29 Lay to their charge guilt upon guilt, *
   and let them not receive your vindication.

30 Let them be wiped out of the book of the living *
   and not be written among the righteous.

31 As for me, I am afflicted and in pain; *
   your help, O God, will lift me up on high.

32 I will praise your Name, O God, in song; *
   I will proclaim your greatness with thanksgiving.

33 This will please you more than an offering of oxen, *
   more than bullocks with horns and hoofs.

34 The afflicted shall see and be glad; *
  those who seek God, their heart shall live.

35 For you, O God, listen to the needy, *
  and your prisoners you do not despise.

36 Let the heavens and the earth praise you, *
  the seas and all that moves in them;

37 For you will save Zion and rebuild the cities of Judah; *
  your people shall live there and have it in possession.

38 The children of your servants will inherit it, *
  and those who love your Name will dwell therein.

Psalm 70

1 Be pleased, O God, to deliver me; *
  O God, make haste to help me.

2 Let those who seek my life be ashamed
  and altogether dismayed; *
    let those who take pleasure in my misfortune,
    draw back and be disgraced.

3 Let those who say to me "Aha!" and gloat over me turn back, *
  because they are ashamed.

4 Let all who seek you rejoice and be glad in you; *
    let those who love your salvation say for ever,
    "Great is the Holy One!"

5 But as for me, I am poor and needy; *
  come to me speedily, O God.

6 You are my helper and my deliverer; *
  O God, do not tarry.

Fourteenth Day: Morning Prayer

PSALM 71

1 In you, O God, have I taken refuge; *
  let me never be ashamed.

2 In your righteousness, deliver me and set me free; *
  incline your ear to me and save me.

3 Be my strong rock, a castle to keep me safe; *
  you are my crag and my stronghold.

4 Deliver me, my God, from the hand of the wicked, *
  from the clutches of the evildoer and the oppressor.

5 For you are my hope, O God, *
  my confidence since I was young.

6 I have been sustained by you ever since I was born;
  from my mother's womb you have been my strength; *
  my praise shall be always of you.

7 I have become a portent to many, *
  but you are my refuge and my strength.

8 Let my mouth be full of your praise *
  and your glory all the day long.

9 Do not cast me off in my old age; *
  forsake me not when my strength fails.

10 For my enemies are talking against me, *
  and those who lie in wait for my life take counsel together.

11 They say that God has forsaken me,
  that they may pursue and seize me, *
    because there is none who will save.

12 O God, be not far from me; *
    come quickly to help me, O my God.

13 Let those who set themselves against me be put to shame
      and be disgraced; *
    let those who seek to do me evil be covered with scorn
      and reproach.

14 But I shall always wait in patience *
    and shall praise you more and more.

15 My mouth shall recount your mighty acts
    and saving deeds all day long, *
      though I cannot know the number of them.

16 I will begin with your mighty works, O God; *
    I will recall your righteousness, yours alone.

17 O God, you have taught me since I was young, *
    and to this day I tell of your wonderful works.

18 And now that I am old and gray-headed, O God,
      do not forsake me, *
    till I make known your strength to this generation
    and your power to all who are to come.

19 Your righteousness, O God, reaches to the heavens; *
    you have done great things;
    who is like you, O God?

20 You have shown me great troubles and adversities, *
    but you will restore my life
    and bring me up again from the deep places of the earth.

21 You strengthen me more and more; *
    you enfold and comfort me;

22 Therefore I will praise you upon the lyre
        for your faithfulness, O my God; *
    I will sing to you with the harp, O Holy One of Israel.

23 My lips will sing with joy when I play to you *
    and so will my soul, which you have redeemed.

24 My tongue will proclaim your righteousness all day long, *
    for they are ashamed and disgraced who sought
        to do me harm.

PSALM 72

1 Give the King your justice, O God, *
    and your righteousness to the King's Son,

2 That he may rule your people righteously *
    and the poor with justice;

3 That the mountains may bring prosperity to the people, *
    and the little hills bring righteousness.

4 He shall defend the needy among the people; *
    he shall rescue the poor and crush the oppressor.

5 He shall live as long as the sun and moon endure, *
    from one generation to another.

6 He shall come down like rain upon the mown field, *
    like showers that water the earth.

7 In his time shall the righteous flourish; *
    there shall be abundance of peace till the moon shall
        be no more.

8 He shall rule from sea to sea *
    and from the River to the ends of the earth.

9 His foes shall bow down before him, *
    and his enemies lick the dust.

10 The rulers of Tarshish and of the isles shall pay tribute, *
    and the rulers of Arabia and Saba offer gifts.

11 All rulers shall bow down before him, *
    and all the nations do him service.

12 For he shall deliver the poor who cries out in distress *
    and the oppressed who has no helper.

13 He shall have pity on the lowly and poor; *
    he shall preserve the lives of the needy.

14 He shall redeem their lives from oppression and violence, *
    and dear shall their blood be in his sight.

15 Long may he live;
    and may there be given to him gold from Arabia; *
        may prayer be made for him always,
        and may they bless him all the day long.

16 May there be abundance of grain on the earth,
   growing thick even on the hilltops; *
      may its fruit flourish like Lebanon,
      and its grain like grass upon the earth.

17 May his Name remain for ever
   and be established as long as the sun endures; *
      may all the nations bless themselves in him and
         call him blest.

18 Blest are you, O God of Israel; *
      you alone do wondrous deeds!

19 And blest is your glorious Name for ever! *
      May all the earth be filled with your glory.
      Amen. Amen.

BOOK THREE

PSALM 73

1 Truly, God is good to Israel, *
     to those who are pure in heart.

2 But as for me, my feet had nearly slipped; *
     I had almost tripped and fallen,

3 Because I envied the proud *
     and saw the prosperity of the wicked:

4 For they suffer no pain, *
     and their bodies are sleek and sound;

5 In the misfortunes of others they have no share; *
     they are not afflicted as others are;

6 Therefore they wear their pride like a necklace *
     and wrap their violence about them like a cloak.

7 Their iniquity comes from gross minds, *
     and their hearts overflow with wicked thoughts.

8 They scoff and speak maliciously; *
     out of their haughtiness they plan oppression.

9 They set their mouths against the heavens, *
     and their evil speech runs through the world.

10 And so the people turn to them *
      and find in them no fault.

11 They say, "How should God know; *
    is there knowledge in the Most High?"

12 So then, these are the wicked; *
    always at ease, they increase their wealth.

13 In vain have I kept my heart clean *
    and washed my hands in innocence.

14 I have been afflicted all day long *
    and punished every morning.

15 Had I gone on speaking this way, *
    I should have betrayed the generation of your children.

16 When I tried to understand these things, *
    it was too hard for me,

17 Until I entered the sanctuary of God *
    and discerned the end of the wicked.

18 Surely, you set them in slippery places; *
    you cast them down in ruin.

19 Oh, how suddenly do they come to destruction, *
    come to an end, and perish from terror!

20 Like a dream when one awakens, O God, *
    when you arise you will make their image vanish.

21 When my mind became embittered, *
    I was sorely wounded in my heart.

22 I was stupid and had no understanding; *
    I was like a brute beast in your presence.

23 Yet I am always with you; *
   you hold me by my right hand.

24 You will guide me by your counsel, *
   and afterwards receive me with glory.

25 Whom have I in heaven but you? *
   And having you I desire nothing upon earth.

26 Though my flesh and my heart should waste away, *
   God is the strength of my heart and my portion for ever.

27 Truly, those who forsake you will perish; *
   you destroy all who are unfaithful.

28 But it is good for me to be near God; *
   I have made the Most High my refuge.

29 I will speak of all your works *
   in the gates of the city of Zion.

PSALM 74

1 O God, why have you utterly cast us off; *
   why is your wrath so hot against the sheep of your pasture?

2 Remember your congregation that you purchased long ago, *
   the tribe you redeemed to be your inheritance,
   and Mount Zion where you dwell.

3 Turn your steps toward the endless ruins; *
   the enemy has laid waste everything in your sanctuary.

4 Your adversaries roared in your holy place; *
   they set up their banners as tokens of victory.

5 They were like men coming up with axes to a grove of trees; *
    they broke down all your carved work with hatchets
        and hammers.

6 They set fire to your holy place; *
    they defiled the dwelling-place of your Name
    and razed it to the ground.

7 They said to themselves, "Let us destroy them altogether." *
    They burned down all the meeting-places of God
        in the land.

8 There are no signs for us to see;
    there is no prophet left; *
    there is not one among us who knows how long.

9 How long, O God, will the adversary scoff; *
    will the enemy blaspheme your Name for ever?

10 Why do you draw back your hand; *
    why is your right hand hidden in your bosom?

11 Yet God is my Sovereign from ancient times, *
    victorious in the midst of the earth.

12 You divided the sea by your might *
    and shattered the heads of the dragons upon the waters;

13 You crushed the heads of Leviathan, *
    which you gave to the people of the desert for food.

14 You split open spring and torrent; *
    you dried up ever-flowing rivers.

15 Yours is the day, yours also the night; *
    you established the moon and the sun.

16 You fixed all the boundaries of the earth; *
    you made both summer and winter.

17 Remember, O God, how the enemy scoffed, *
    how a foolish people despised your Name.

18 Do not hand over the life of your dove to wild beasts; *
    never forget the lives of your poor.

19 Look upon your covenant; *
    the dark places of the earth are haunts of violence.

20 Let not the oppressed turn away ashamed; *
    let the poor and needy praise your Name.

21 Arise, O God, maintain your cause; *
    remember how fools revile you all day long.

22 Forget not the clamor of your adversaries, *
    the unending tumult of those who rise up against you.

Fifteenth Day: Morning Prayer

PSALM 75

1 We give you thanks, O God, we give you thanks, *
    calling upon your Name and declaring all your
        wonderful deeds.

2 "I will appoint a time," says God; *
    "I will judge with equity.

3 Though the earth and all its inhabitants are quaking, *
    I will make its pillars fast.

4 I will say to the boasters, 'Boast no more,' *
    and to the wicked, 'Do not toss your horns;

5 Do not toss your horns so high, *
    nor speak with a proud neck.'

6 For judgment is neither from the east nor from the west, *
    nor yet from the wilderness or the mountains."

7 You are judge, O God; *
    you put down one and lift up another.

8 For in your hand there is a cup,
    full of spiced and foaming wine, which you pour out, *
    and all the wicked of the earth shall drink and
        drain the dregs.

9 But I will rejoice for ever; *
    I will sing praises to you, O God of Jacob.

10 For you will break off all the horns of the wicked, *
    but the horns of the righteous shall be exalted.

PSALM 76

1 In Judah you are known, O God; *
    your Name is great in Israel.

2 At Salem is your tabernacle, *
    and your dwelling is in Zion.

3 There you broke the flashing arrows, *
    the shield, the sword, and the weapons of battle.

4 How glorious you are, *
    more splendid than the everlasting mountains!

5 The strong of heart have been despoiled;
   they sink into sleep; *
      none of the warriors can lift a hand.

6 At your rebuke, O God of Jacob, *
      both horse and rider lie stunned.

7 What terror you inspire; *
      who can stand before you when you are angry?

8 From heaven you pronounced judgment; *
      the earth was afraid and was still,

9 When God rose up to judgment *
      and to save all the oppressed of the earth.

10 Truly, wrathful Edom will give you thanks, *
      and the remnant of Hamath will keep your feasts.

11 Make a vow to your God and keep it; *
      let the nations bring gifts to the One who is worthy
         to be feared,

12 Who breaks the spirit of princes, *
      and strikes terror in the rulers of the earth.

Psalm 77

1 I will cry aloud to God; *
      I cry aloud to the One who will hear me.

2 In the day of my trouble I sought after God; *
      my hands were stretched out by night and did not tire;
      I refused to be comforted.

3 I think of God; I am restless; *
    I ponder and my spirit faints.

4 You will not let my eyelids close; *
    I am troubled and I cannot speak.

5 I consider the days of old; *
    I remember the years long past;

6 I commune with my heart in the night; *
    I ponder and search my mind.

7 Will you cast me off for ever; *
    will you no more show your favor?

8 Has your loving-kindness come to an end for ever; *
    has your promise failed for evermore?

9 Have you forgotten to be gracious; *
    have you, in your anger, withheld your compassion?

10 And I said, "My grief is this: *
    the right hand of the Most High has lost its power."

11 I will remember the works of God *
    and call to mind your wonders of old time.

12 I will meditate on all your acts *
    and ponder your mighty deeds.

13 Your way, O God, is holy; *
    who is so great a god as our God?

14 You are the God who works wonders *
    and have declared your power among the peoples.

15 By your strength you have redeemed your people, *
 the children of Jacob and Joseph.

16 The waters saw you, O God;
 the waters saw you and trembled; *
  the very depths were shaken.

17 The clouds poured out water;
 the skies thundered; *
  your arrows flashed to and fro;

18 The sound of your thunder was in the whirlwind;
 your lightnings lit up the world; *
  the earth trembled and shook.

19 Your way was in the sea,
 and your paths in the great waters, *
  yet your footsteps were not seen.

20 You led your people like a flock, *
 by the hand of Moses and Aaron.

Fifteenth Day: Evening Prayer

Psalm 78

Part I

1 Hear my teaching, O my people; *
 incline your ears to the words of my mouth.

2 I will open my mouth in a parable; *
 I will declare the mysteries of ancient times.

3 That which we have heard and known,
  and what our forebears have told us, *
    we will not hide from their children.

4 We will recount to generations to come
  your praiseworthy deeds and your power, O God, *
    and the wonderful works you have done.

5 You gave your decrees to Jacob
  and established a law for Israel, *
    which you commanded them to teach their children;

6 That the generations to come might know,
  and the children yet unborn, *
    that they in their turn might tell it to their children;

7 So that they might put their trust in you *
    and not forget your deeds,
    but keep your commandments;

8 And not be like their forebears,
  a stubborn and rebellious generation, *
    a generation whose heart was not steadfast
    and whose spirit was not faithful to you.

9 The people of Ephraim, armed with the bow, *
    turned back in the day of battle;

10 They did not keep your covenant *
    and refused to walk in your law;

11 They forgot what you had done *
    and the wonders you had shown them.

12 You worked marvels in the sight of their forebears, *
    in the land of Egypt, in the field of Zoan.

13 You split open the sea and let them pass through; *
   you made the waters stand up like walls.

14 You led them with a cloud by day *
   and all the night through with a glow of fire.

15 You split the hard rocks in the wilderness *
   and gave them drink as from the great deep.

16 You brought streams out of the cliff, *
   and the waters gushed out like rivers.

17 But they went on sinning against you, *
   rebelling in the desert against the Most High.

18 They tested you in their hearts, *
   demanding food for their craving.

19 They railed against you and said, *
   "Can God set a table in the wilderness?

20 True, God struck the rock,
   the waters gushed out, and the gullies overflowed; *
   but is God able to give bread
   or to provide meat for the people?"

21 When you heard this, you were full of wrath; *
   a fire was kindled against Jacob,
   and your anger mounted against Israel;

22 For they had no faith in you, *
   nor did they put their trust in your saving power.

23 So you commanded the clouds above *
   and opened the doors of heaven.

24 You rained down manna upon them to eat *
   and gave them grain from heaven.

25 So mortals ate the bread of angels; *
   you provided for them food enough.

26 You caused the east wind to blow in the heavens *
   and led out the south wind by your might.

27 You rained down flesh upon them like dust *
   and winged birds like the sand of the sea.

28 You let it fall in the midst of their camp *
   and round about their dwellings.

29 So they ate and were well filled, *
   for you gave them what they craved.

30 But they did not stop their craving, *
   though the food was still in their mouths.

31 So your anger mounted against them; *
   you slew the strongest among them
   and laid low the youth of Israel.

32 In spite of all this, they went on sinning *
   and had no faith in your wonderful works.

33 So you brought their days to an end like a breath *
   and their years in sudden terror.

34 Whenever you slew them, they would seek you *
   and repent, and diligently search for you.

35 They would remember that you were their rock, *
   that you, the Most High, were their redeemer.

36 But they flattered you with their mouths *
    and lied to you with their tongues.

37 Their heart was not steadfast toward you, *
    and they were not faithful to your covenant.

38 But you were so merciful that you forgave their sins
    and did not destroy them; *
        many times you held back your anger
        and did not permit your wrath to be roused.

39 For you remembered that they were but flesh, *
    a breath that goes forth and does not return.

PSALM 78: PART II

40 How often the people disobeyed you in the wilderness *
    and offended you in the desert!

41 Again and again they tempted you *
    and provoked you, the Holy One of Israel.

42 They did not remember your power *
    in the day when you ransomed them from the enemy;

43 How you wrought your signs in Egypt *
    and your omens in the field of Zoan.

44 You turned their rivers into blood, *
    so that they could not drink of their streams.

45 You sent swarms of flies among them, which ate them up, *
    and frogs, which destroyed them.

46 You gave their crops to the caterpillar, *
    the fruit of their toil to the locust.

47 You killed their vines with hail *
    and their sycamores with frost.

48 You delivered their cattle to hailstones *
    and their livestock to hot thunderbolts.

49 You poured out upon them your blazing anger: *
    fury, indignation, and distress,
    a troop of destroying angels.

50 You gave full rein to your anger;
    you did not spare their souls from death, *
    but delivered their lives to the plague.

51 You struck down all the firstborn of Egypt, *
    the first-fruits of their strength in the dwellings of Ham.

52 You led out your people like sheep *
    and guided them in the wilderness like a flock.

53 You led them to safety, and they were not afraid; *
    but the sea overwhelmed their enemies.

54 You brought them to your holy land, *
    the mountain your right hand had won.

55 You drove out the Canaanites before them
    and apportioned an inheritance to them by lot; *
    you made the tribes of Israel to dwell in their tents.

56 But they tested you, O Most High, and defied you *
    and did not keep your commandments.

57 They turned away and were disloyal like their forebears; *
    they were undependable like a warped bow.

58 They grieved you with their hill-altars *
    and provoked your displeasure with their idols.

59 When you heard this, you were angry *
    and utterly rejected Israel.

60 You forsook the shrine at Shiloh, *
    the tabernacle where you had lived among your people.

61 You delivered the ark into captivity, *
    your glory into the adversary's hand.

62 You gave your people to the sword *
    and were angered against your inheritance.

63 The fire consumed their young men; *
    there were no wedding songs for their maidens.

64 Their priests fell by the sword, *
    and their widows made no lamentation.

65 Then you awoke, O God, as though from sleep, *
    like a warrior refreshed with wine.

66 You struck your enemies on the backside *
    and put them to perpetual shame.

67 You rejected the tent of Joseph *
    and did not choose the tribe of Ephraim;

68 You chose instead the tribe of Judah *
    and Mount Zion, which you loved.

69 You built your sanctuary like the heights of heaven, *
    like the earth which you founded for ever.

70 You chose David your servant *
    and took him away from the sheepfolds.

71 You brought him from following the ewes, *
    to be a shepherd over Jacob your people
    and over Israel your inheritance.

72 So he shepherded them with a faithful and true heart, *
    and guided them with the skillfulness of his hands.

Sixteenth Day: Morning Prayer

PSALM 79

1 O God, the nations have come into your inheritance;
    they have profaned your holy temple; *
      they have made Jerusalem a heap of rubble.

2 They have given the bodies of your servants as food for
      the birds of the air, *
    and the flesh of your faithful ones to the beasts
      of the field.

3 They have shed their blood like water on every side
      of Jerusalem, *
    and there was no one to bury them.

4 We have become a reproach to our neighbors, *
    an object of scorn and derision to those around us.

5 How long will you be angry, O God; *
    will your fury blaze like fire for ever?

6 Pour out your wrath upon the nations who have
        not known you *
    and upon the realms that have not called upon
        your Name.

7 For they have devoured Jacob *
    and made his dwelling a ruin.

8 Remember not our past sins;
    let your compassion be swift to meet us; *
    for we have been brought very low.

9 Help us, O God our Savior, for the glory of your Name; *
    deliver us and forgive us our sins, for your Name's sake.

10 Why should the nations say, "Where is their God?" *
    Let it be known among the nations and in our sight
    that you avenge the shedding of your servants' blood.

11 Let the sorrowful sighing of the prisoners come before you, *
    and by your great might spare those who are
        condemned to die.

12 May the revilings with which they reviled you, O God, *
    return seven-fold into their bosoms.

13 For we are your people and the sheep of your pasture; *
    we will give you thanks for ever
    and show forth your praise from age to age.

PSALM 80

1 Hear, O Shepherd of Israel, leading Joseph like a flock; *
    shine forth, you that are enthroned upon the cherubim.

2 In the presence of Ephraim, Benjamin, and Manasseh, *
    stir up your strength and come to help us.

3 Restore us, O God of hosts; *
    show the light of your countenance, and we shall be saved.

4 O God of hosts, *
    how long will you be angered
    despite the prayers of your people?

5 You have fed them with the bread of tears; *
    you have given them bowls of tears to drink.

6 You have made us the derision of our neighbors, *
    and our enemies laugh us to scorn.

7 Restore us, O God of hosts; *
    show the light of your countenance, and we shall be saved.

8 You have brought a vine out of Egypt; *
    you cast out the nations and planted it.

9 You prepared the ground for it; *
    it took root and filled the land.

10 The mountains were covered by its shadow *
    and the towering cedar trees by its boughs.

11 You stretched out its tendrils to the Sea *
    and its branches to the River.

12 Why have you broken down its wall, *
    so that all who pass by pluck off its grapes?

13 The wild boar of the forest has ravaged it, *
    and the beasts of the field have grazed upon it.

14 Turn now, O God of hosts, look down from heaven;
behold and tend this vine; *
   preserve what your right hand has planted.

15 They burn it with fire like rubbish; *
   at the rebuke of your countenance let them perish.

16 Let your hand be upon the one at your right hand, *
   those whom you have made so strong for yourself.

17 And so will we never turn away from you, *
   give us life, that we may call upon your Name.

18 Restore us, O God of hosts; *
   show the light of your countenance, and we shall be saved.

PSALM 81

1 Sing with joy to God our strength, *
   and raise a loud shout to the God of Jacob.

2 Raise a song and sound the timbrel, *
   the merry harp, and the lyre.

3 Blow the ram's-horn at the new moon *
   and at the full moon, the day of our feast.

4 For this is a statute for Israel, *
   a law of the God of Jacob.

5 God laid it as a solemn charge upon Joseph, *
   when he came out of the land of Egypt.

6 I heard an unfamiliar voice saying, *
   "I eased Israel's shoulder from the burden;
   their hands were set free from bearing the load."

7 You called on me in trouble, and I saved you; *
    I answered you from the secret place of thunder
    and tested you at the waters of Meribah.

8 Hear, O my people, and I will admonish you: *
    O Israel, if you would but listen to me!

9 There shall be no strange god among you; *
    you shall not worship a foreign god.

10 I am your God,
    who brought you out of the land of Egypt and said, *
    "Open your mouth wide, and I will fill it."

11 And yet my people did not hear my voice, *
    and Israel would not obey me.

12 So I gave them over to the stubbornness of their hearts, *
    to follow their own devices.

13 Oh, that my people would listen to me, *
    that Israel would walk in my ways!

14 I should soon subdue their enemies *
    and turn my hand against their foes.

15 Those who hate me would cringe before me, *
    and their punishment would last for ever.

16 But Israel would I feed with the finest wheat *
    and satisfy them with honey from the rock.

PSALM 82

1 God stands in the council of heaven *
    and gives judgment in the midst of the gods:

2 "How long will you judge unjustly *
    and show favor to the wicked?

3 Save the weak and the orphan; *
    defend the humble and needy;

4 Rescue the weak and the poor; *
    deliver them from the power of the wicked.

5 They do not know, neither do they understand;
    they go about in darkness; *
    all the foundations of the earth are shaken.

6 Now I say to you, 'You are gods, *
    and all of you children of the Most High;

7 Nevertheless, you shall die like mortals *
    and fall like any ruler.' "

8 Arise, O God, and rule the earth, *
    for you shall take all nations for your own.

PSALM 83

1 O God, do not be silent; *
    do not keep still nor hold your peace, O God;

2 For your enemies are in tumult, *
    and those who hate you have lifted up their heads.

3 They take secret counsel against your people *
　　and plot against those whom you protect.

4 They have said, "Come, let us wipe them out from
　　　　　among the nations; *
　　let the name of Israel be remembered no more."

5 They have conspired together; *
　　they have made an alliance against you:

6 The tents of Edom and the Ishmaelites; *
　　the Moabites and the Hagarenes;

7 Gebal, and Ammon, and Amalek; *
　　the Philistines and those who dwell in Tyre.

8 The Assyrians also have joined them *
　　and have come to help the people of Lot.

9 Do to them as you did to Midian, *
　　to Sisera, and to Jabin at the river of Kishon:

10 They were destroyed at Endor; *
　　they became like dung upon the ground.

11 Make their leaders like Oreb and Zeëb, *
　　and all their commanders like Zebah and Zalmunna,

12 Who said, "Let us take for ourselves *
　　the fields of God as our possession."

13 O my God, make them like whirling dust *
　　and like chaff before the wind,

14 Like fire that burns down a forest, *
　　like the flame that sets mountains ablaze.

15 Drive them with your tempest *
    and terrify them with your storm;

16 Cover their faces with shame, O God, *
    that they may seek your Name.

17 Let them be disgraced and terrified for ever; *
    let them be put to confusion and perish.

18 Let them know that you, whose Name is Holy, *
    you alone are the Most High over all the earth.

PSALM 84

1 How dear to me is your dwelling, O God of hosts! *
    My soul has a desire and longing for your courts;
    my heart and my flesh rejoice in the living God.

2 The sparrow has found her a house
  and the swallow a nest where she may lay her young, *
    by the side of your altars, O God of hosts,
    my Ruler and my God.

3 Happy are they who dwell in your house; *
    they will always be praising you.

4 Happy are the people whose strength is in you, *
    whose hearts are set on the pilgrims' way.

5 Those who go through the desolate valley will find
    it a place of springs, *
    for the early rains have covered it with pools of water.

6 They will climb from height to height; *
    the God of gods will be revealed in Zion.

7 O God of hosts, hear my prayer; *
hearken, O God of Jacob.

8 Behold our defender, O God, *
and look upon the face of your Anointed,

9 For one day in your courts is better than
a thousand in my own room, *
and to stand at the threshold of the house of my God
than to dwell in the tents of the wicked;

10 For God is both sun and shield *
and will give grace and glory.

11 No good thing will God withhold *
from those who walk with integrity.

12 O God of hosts, *
happy are they who put their trust in you!

PSALM 85

1 You have been gracious to your land, O God;*
you have restored the good fortune of Jacob.

2 You have forgiven the iniquity of your people *
and blotted out all their sins.

3 You have withdrawn all your fury *
and turned yourself from your wrathful indignation.

4 Restore us then, O God our Savior; *
let your anger depart from us.

5 Will you be displeased with us for ever; *
will you prolong your anger from age to age?

6 Will you not give us life again, *
  that your people may rejoice in you?

7 Show us your mercy, O God, *
  and grant us your salvation.

8 I will listen to what you are saying, *
  for you are speaking peace to your faithful people
  and to those who turn their hearts to you.

9 Truly, your salvation is very near to those who fear you, *
  that your glory may dwell in our land.

10 Mercy and truth have met together; *
  righteousness and peace have kissed each other.

11 Truth shall spring up from the earth, *
  and righteousness shall look down from heaven.

12 You, O God, will indeed grant prosperity, *
  and our land will yield its increase.

13 Righteousness shall go before you, *
  and peace shall be a pathway for your feet.

Seventeenth Day: Morning Prayer

PSALM 86

1 Bow down your ear, O God, and answer me, *
  for I am poor and in misery.

2 Keep watch over my life, for I am faithful; *
  save your servant, for I put my trust in you.

3 Be merciful to me, O God, for you are my God; *
    I call upon you all the day long.

4 Gladden the soul of your servant, *
    for to you, O God, I lift up my soul.

5 For you, O God, are good and forgiving, *
    and great is your love toward all who call upon you.

6 Give ear, O God, to my prayer, *
    and attend to the voice of my supplications.

7 In the time of my trouble I will call upon you, *
    for you will answer me.

8 Among the gods there is none like you, O God, *
    nor anything like your works.

9 All nations you have made will come and worship you,
        O God, *
    and glorify your Name.

10 For you are great; you do wondrous things; *
    and you alone are God.

11 Teach me your way, O God, and I will walk in your truth; *
    knit my heart to you that I may fear your Name.

12 I will thank you, my God, with all my heart, *
    and glorify your Name for evermore.

13 For great is your love toward me; *
    you have delivered me from the nethermost Pit.

14 The arrogant rise up against me, O God,
    and a band of the violent seeks my life; *
        they have not set you before their eyes.

15 But you, O God, are gracious and full of compassion, *
    slow to anger, and full of kindness and truth.

16 Turn to me and have mercy upon me; *
    give your strength to your servant
    and save the child of your handmaid.

17 Show me a sign of your favor,
    so that those who hate me may see it and be ashamed, *
    because you, O God, have helped me and comforted me.

PSALM 87

1 On the holy mountain stands the city God has founded; *
    God loves the gates of Zion
    more than all the dwellings of Jacob.

2 Glorious things are spoken of you, *
    O city of our God.

3 I count Egypt and Babylon among those who know me; *
    behold Philistia, Tyre, and Ethiopia:
    in Zion were they born.

4 Of Zion it shall be said, "Everyone was born there, *
    and the Most High God shall sustain it."

5 God will record in the roll of the peoples, *
    "These also were born there."

6 The singers and the dancers will say, *
    "All my fresh springs are in you."

Psalm 88

1 O my God, my Savior, *
    by day and night I cry to you.

2 Let my prayer enter into your presence; *
    incline your ear to my lamentation.

3 For I am full of trouble; *
    my life is at the brink of the grave.

4 I am counted among those who go down to the Pit; *
    I have become like one who has no strength;

5 Lost among the dead, *
    like the slain who lie in the grave,

6 Whom you remember no more, *
    for they are cut off from your hand.

7 You have laid me in the depths of the Pit, *
    in dark places, and in the abyss.

8 Your anger weighs upon me heavily, *
    and all your great waves overwhelm me.

9 You have put my friends far from me;
  you have made me to be abhorred by them; *
    I am in prison and cannot get free.

10 My sight has failed me because of trouble; *
    O God, I have called upon you daily;
    I have stretched out my hands to you.

11 Do you work wonders for the dead; *
    will those who have died stand up and give you thanks?

12 Will your loving-kindness be declared in the grave *
    or your faithfulness in the land of destruction?

13 Will your wonders be known in the dark *
    or your righteousness in the country where all is forgotten?

14 But as for me, O God, I cry to you for help; *
    in the morning my prayer comes before you.

15 O God, why have you rejected me; *
    why have you hidden your face from me?

16 Ever since my youth, I have been wretched and at the
        point of death; *
    I have borne your terrors with a troubled mind.

17 Your blazing anger has swept over me; *
    your terrors have destroyed me;

18 They surround me all day long like a flood; *
    they encompass me on every side.

19 My friend and my neighbor you have put away from me, *
    and darkness is my only companion.

Seventeenth Day: Evening Prayer

Psalm 89

Part I

1 Your love, O God, for ever will I sing; *
    from age to age my mouth will proclaim your faithfulness.

2 For I am persuaded that your love is established for ever; *
   you have set your faithfulness firmly in the heavens.

3 "I have made a covenant with my chosen one; *
   I have sworn an oath to David my servant:

4 'I will establish your line for ever, *
   and preserve your throne for all generations.' "

5 The heavens bear witness to your wonders, O God, *
   and to your faithfulness in the assembly of the holy ones;

6 For who in the skies can be compared to you, O God; *
   who is like you among the gods?

7 You are much to be feared in the council of the holy ones, *
   great and terrible to all those round about you.

8 Who is like you, O God of hosts? *
   O Mighty One, your faithfulness is all around you.

9 You rule the raging of the sea *
   and still the surging of its waves.

10 You have crushed Rahab of the deep with a deadly wound; *
   you have scattered your enemies with your mighty arm.

11 Yours are the heavens; the earth also is yours; *
   you laid the foundations of the world and all that is in it.

12 You have made the north and the south; *
   Tabor and Hermon rejoice in your Name.

13 You have a mighty arm; *
   strong is your hand and high is your right hand.

14 Righteousness and justice are the foundations
            of your throne; *
    love and truth go before your face.

15 Happy are the people who know the festal shout; *
    they walk, O God, in the light of your presence.

16 They rejoice daily in your Name; *
    they are jubilant in your righteousness.

17 For you are the glory of their strength, *
    and by your favor our might is exalted.

18 Truly, God is our Ruler; *
    the Holy One of Israel is our Sovereign.

PSALM 89: PART II

19 You spoke once in a vision and said to your faithful people: *
    "I have set the crown upon a warrior
    and have exalted one chosen out of the people.

20 I have found David my servant; *
    with my holy oil have I anointed him.

21 My hand will hold him fast, *
    and my arm will make him strong.

22 No enemy shall deceive him *
    nor any adversary bring him down.

23 I will crush his foes before him *
    and strike down those who hate him.

24 My faithfulness and love shall be with him, *
    and he shall be victorious through my Name.

25 I shall make his dominion extend *
      from the Great Sea to the River.

26 He will say to me, 'You are my Creator, *
      my God and the rock of my salvation.'

27 I will make him my firstborn *
      and higher than the rulers of the earth.

28 I will keep my love for him for ever, *
      and my covenant will stand firm for him.

29 I will establish his line for ever *
      and his throne as the days of heaven."

30 "If his children forsake my law *
      and do not walk according to my judgments;

31 If they break my statutes *
      and do not keep my commandments;

32 I will punish their transgressions with a rod *
      and their iniquities with the lash;

33 But I will not take my love from him *
      nor let my faithfulness prove false.

34 I will not break my covenant *
      nor change what has gone out of my lips.

35 Once for all I have sworn by my holiness: *
      'I will not lie to David.

36 His line shall endure for ever *
      and his throne as the sun before me;

37 It shall stand fast for evermore like the moon, *
   the abiding witness in the sky.' "

38 But you have cast off and rejected your anointed; *
   you have become enraged at him.

39 You have broken your covenant with your servant, *
   defiled his crown, and hurled it to the ground.

40 You have breached all his walls *
   and laid his strongholds in ruins.

41 All who pass by despoil him; *
   he has become the scorn of his neighbors.

42 You have exalted the right hand of his foes *
   and made all his enemies rejoice.

43 You have turned back the edge of his sword *
   and have not sustained him in battle.

44 You have put an end to his splendor *
   and cast his throne to the ground.

45 You have cut short the days of his youth *
   and have covered him with shame.

46 How long will you hide yourself, O God,
   will you hide yourself for ever; *
   how long will your anger burn like fire?

47 Remember, O God, how short life is, *
   how frail you have made all flesh.

48 Who can live and not see death; *
   who can be saved from the power of the grave?

49 Where, O God, are your loving-kindnesses of old, *
    which you promised David in your faithfulness?

50 Remember how your servant is mocked, *
    how I carry in my bosom the taunts of many peoples,

51 The taunts your enemies have hurled, O God, *
    which they hurled at the heels of your anointed.

52 Blessed be God for evermore! *
    Amen, I say, Amen.

BOOK FOUR

Eighteenth Day: Morning Prayer

PSALM 90

1 O God, you have been our refuge *
  from one generation to another.

2 Before the mountains were brought forth,
  or the land and the earth were born, *
  from age to age you are God.

3 You turn us back to the dust and say, *
  "Go back, O child of earth."

4 For a thousand years in your sight are like yesterday
      when it is past *
  and like a watch in the night.

5 You sweep us away like a dream; *
  we fade away suddenly like the grass.

6 In the morning it is green and flourishes; *
  in the evening it is dried up and withered.

7 For we consume away in your displeasure; *
  we are afraid because of your wrathful indignation.

8 Our iniquities you have set before you *
  and our secret sins in the light of your countenance.

9 When you are angry, all our days are gone; *
  we bring our years to an end like a sigh.

10 The span of our life is seventy years,
  perhaps in strength even eighty; *
    yet the sum of them is but labor and sorrow,
    for they pass away quickly and we are gone.

11 Who regards the power of your wrath; *
  who rightly fears your indignation?

12 So teach us to number our days *
  that we may apply our hearts to wisdom.

13 Return, O God; how long will you tarry? *
  Be gracious to your servants.

14 Satisfy us by your loving-kindness in the morning; *
  so shall we rejoice and be glad all the days of our life.

15 Make us glad by the measure of the days that you afflicted us *
  and the years in which we suffered adversity.

16 Show your servants your works *
  and your splendor to their children.

17 May the graciousness of our God be upon us; *
  prosper the work of our hands;
  prosper our handiwork.

Psalm 91

1 They who dwell in the shelter of the Most High *
  abide under the shadow of the Almighty.

2 They shall say to God, "You are my refuge and
      my stronghold, *
  my God in whom I put my trust."

3 For God shall deliver you from the snare of the hunter *
   and from the deadly pestilence.

4 God's pinions shall cover you,
  and under God's wings you shall find refuge; *
   God's faithfulness shall be a shield and buckler.

5 You shall not be afraid of any terror by night *
   nor of the arrow that flies by day;

6 Of the plague that stalks in the darkness *
   nor of the sickness that lays waste at mid-day.

7 A thousand shall fall at your side
  and ten thousand at your right hand, *
   but it shall not come near you.

8 Your eyes have only to behold, *
   to see the reward of the wicked.

9 Because you have made God your refuge *
   and the Most High your habitation,

10 There shall no evil happen to you, *
   neither shall any plague come near your dwelling.

11 For God shall give the angels charge over you, *
   to keep you in all your ways.

12 They shall bear you in their hands, *
   lest you dash your foot against a stone.

13 You shall tread upon the lion and adder; *
   you shall trample the young lion and the serpent
      under your feet.

14 Because you are bound to me in love,
    therefore will I deliver you; *
        I will protect you, because you know my Name.

15 You shall call upon me, and I will answer you; *
    I am with you in trouble; I will rescue you and
        bring you honor.

16 With long life will I satisfy you *
    and show you my salvation.

Psalm 92

1 It is a good thing to give thanks to God *
    and to sing praises to your Name, O Most High;

2 To tell of your loving-kindness early in the morning *
    and of your faithfulness in the night season;

3 On the psaltery, and on the lyre, *
    and to the melody of the harp,

4 For you have made me glad by your acts, O God, *
    and I shout for joy because of the works of your hands.

5 O God, how great are your works; *
    your thoughts are very deep.

6 The dullard does not know
  nor does the fool understand, *
        that though the wicked grow like weeds
        and all the workers of iniquity flourish,

7 They flourish only to be destroyed for ever; *
    but you, O God, are exalted for evermore.

8 For lo, your enemies, O God,
   lo, your enemies shall perish, *
      and all the workers of iniquity shall be scattered.

9 But my horn you have exalted like the horns of wild bulls; *
      I am anointed with fresh oil.

10 My eyes also gloat over my enemies, *
      and my ears rejoice to hear the doom of
         the wicked who rise up against me.

11 The righteous shall flourish like a palm tree *
      and shall spread abroad like a cedar of Lebanon.

12 Those who are planted in the house of God *
      shall flourish in the heavenly courts.

13 They shall still bear fruit in old age; *
      they shall be green and succulent,

14 That they may show how upright God is, *
      my Rock, in whom there is no fault.

Eighteenth Day: Evening Prayer

PSALM 93

1 God is Sovereign,
   clothed in splendid apparel; *
      God is robed in majesty
      and is girded with strength.

2 God has made the whole world so sure *
      that it cannot be moved;

3 Ever since the world began,
  your throne has been established; *
    you are from everlasting.

4 The waters have lifted up, O God,
  the waters have lifted up their voice; *
    the waters have lifted up their pounding waves.

5 Mightier than the sound of many waters,
  mightier than the breakers of the sea, *
    mightier is the Holy One who dwells on high.

6 Your testimonies are very sure, *
    and holiness adorns your house, O God,
    for ever and for evermore.

PSALM 94

1 O mighty God of vengeance, *
    O God of vengeance, show yourself.

2 Rise up, O Judge of the world; *
    give the arrogant their just deserts.

3 How long shall the wicked, O God, *
    how long shall the wicked triumph?

4 They bluster in their insolence; *
    all evildoers are full of boasting.

5 They crush your people, O God, *
    and afflict your chosen nation.

6 They murder the widow and the stranger *
    and put the orphans to death.

7 Yet they say, "God does not see, *
    the God of Jacob takes no notice."

8 Consider well, you dullards among the people; *
    when will you fools understand?

9 Does the one who planted the ear not hear; *
    does the one who formed the eye not see?

10 Will the one who admonishes the nations not punish; *
    does the one who teaches all the world have no knowledge?

11 God knows our human thoughts, *
    how like a puff of wind they are.

12 Happy are they whom you instruct, O God, *
    whom you teach out of your law,

13 To give them rest in evil days, *
    until a pit is dug for the wicked.

14 For you will not abandon your people *
    nor will you forsake your own.

15 For judgment will again be just, *
    and all the true of heart will follow it.

16 Who rose up for me against the wicked; *
    who took my part against the evildoers?

17 If you had not come to my help, *
    I should soon have dwelt in the land of silence.

18 As often as I said, "My foot has slipped," *
    your love, O God, upheld me.

19 When many cares fill my mind, *
   your consolations cheer my soul.

20 Can a corrupt tribunal have any part with you, *
   one which frames evil into law?

21 They conspire against the life of the just *
   and condemn the innocent to death.

22 But you have become my stronghold; *
   you are the rock of my trust.

23 You will turn their wickedness back upon them
   and destroy them in their own malice; *
   you, O Most High, will destroy them.

Nineteenth Day: Morning Prayer

PSALM 95

1 Come, let us sing to the Holy One; *
   let us shout for joy to the Rock of our salvation.

2 Let us come before God's presence with thanksgiving *
   and raise a loud shout with psalms.

3 For you, O God, are a great God; *
   you are great above all gods.

4 In your hand are the caverns of the earth, *
   and the heights of the hills are yours also.

5 The sea is yours, for you made it, *
   and your hands have molded the dry land.

6 Come, let us bow down and bend the knee, *
    and kneel before God, our Maker,

7 For you are our God,
    and we are the people of your pasture and the sheep
        of your hand. *
    Oh, that today we would hearken to your voice!

8 Harden not your hearts,
    as your forebears did in the wilderness, *
        at Meribah, and on that day at Massah,
        when they tempted me;

9 They put me to the test, *
    though they had seen my works.

10 Forty years long I detested that generation and said, *
    "This people are wayward in their hearts;
    they do not know my ways."

11 So I swore in my wrath, *
    "They shall not enter into my rest."

PSALM 96

1 Sing to God a new song; *
    sing to God all the whole earth.

2 Sing and bless God's holy Name; *
    proclaim the good news of salvation from day to day.

3 Declare God's glory among the nations, *
    God's wonders among all peoples.

4 For God is great and greatly to be praised, *
    more to be feared than all gods.

5 As for all the gods of the nations, they are but idols, *
    but it is God who made the heavens.

6 Oh, the majesty and magnificence of God's presence! *
    Oh, the power and the splendor of God's sanctuary!

7 Ascribe to God, you families of the peoples, *
    ascribe to God honor and power.

8 Ascribe due honor to God's holy Name; *
    bring offerings and come into God's courts.

9 Worship the Most High in the beauty of holiness; *
    let the whole earth tremble before God.

10 Tell it out among the nations that God reigns! *
    God has made the world so firm that it cannot be moved,
    and will judge the peoples with equity.

11 Let the heavens rejoice, and let the earth be glad;
    let the sea thunder and all that is in it; *
    let the field be joyful and all that is therein.

12 Then shall all the trees of the wood shout for joy
    before God, who will come, *
    who will come to judge the earth.

13 God will judge the world with righteousness *
    and the peoples with truth.

Psalm 97

1 You reign, O God; let the earth rejoice; *
   let the multitude of the isles be glad.

2 Clouds and darkness are round about you; *
   righteousness and justice are the
         foundations of your throne.

3 A fire goes before you *
   and burns up your enemies on every side.

4 Your lightnings light up the world; *
   the earth sees it and is afraid.

5 The mountains melt like wax at your presence, O God, *
   at your presence, O God of the whole earth.

6 The heavens declare your righteousness, *
   and all the peoples see your glory.

7 Confounded be all who worship carved images
   and delight in false gods! *
   Let all gods bow down before you.

8 Zion hears and is glad, and the cities of Judah rejoice, *
   because of your judgments, O God.

9 For you are God,
   most high over all the earth; *
   you are exalted far above all gods.

10 You love those who hate evil; *
   you preserve the lives of your saints
   and deliver them from the hand of the wicked.

11 Light has sprung up for the righteous *
    and joyful gladness for those who are truehearted.

12 Rejoice in God, you righteous, *
    and give thanks to God's holy Name.

Nineteenth Day: Evening Prayer

Psalm 98

1 Sing a new song to God, *
    who has done marvelous things.

2 With your right hand, O God, and your holy arm, *
    you have won for yourself the victory.

3 You have made known your victory; *
    your righteousness have you openly shown in
        the sight of the nations.

4 You remember your mercy and faithfulness to
        the house of Israel, *
    and all the ends of the earth have seen the
        victory of our God.

5 Shout with joy to God, all you lands; *
    lift up your voice, rejoice, and sing.

6 Sing to God with the harp, *
    with the harp and the voice of song.

7 With trumpets and the sound of the horn, *
    shout with joy before God who reigns in majesty.

8 Let the sea make a noise and all that is in it, *
   the lands and those who dwell therein.

9 Let the rivers clap their hands, *
   and let the hills ring out with joy before God,
   who will come to judge the earth.

10 God shall judge the world in righteousness *
   and the peoples with equity.

Psalm 99

1 God reigns; let the people tremble; *
   God is enthroned upon the cherubim;
   let the earth shake.

2 God is great in Zion *
   and is high above all peoples.

3 Let them confess God's Name, which is great and awesome; *
   God is the Holy One.

4 "O mighty Ruler, lover of justice,
   you have established equity; *
   you have executed justice and righteousness in Jacob."

5 We proclaim your greatness, O God,
   and fall down before your footstool; *
   you are the Holy One.

6 Moses and Aaron among your priests,
   and Samuel among those who call upon your Name, *
   they called upon you, and you answered them.

7 You spoke to them out of the pillar of cloud; *
    they kept your testimonies and the decree that
        you gave them.

8 "O Holy God, you answered them indeed; *
    you were a God who forgave them,
    yet punished them for their evil deeds."

9 Proclaim the greatness of our God,
  and worship on God's holy hill, *
    for our God is the Holy One.

Psalm 100

1 May all lands be joyful before you, O God, *
    serve you with gladness
    and come before your presence with a song.

2 For we know that you are God; *
    you yourself have made us, and we are yours;
    we are your people and the sheep of your pasture.

3 We shall enter your gates with thanksgiving,
  go into your courts with praise, *
    give thanks to you and call upon your Name.

4 For you are good;
  your mercy is everlasting, *
    and your faithfulness endures from age to age.

Psalm 101

1 I will sing of mercy and justice; *
    to you, O God, will I sing praises.

2 I will strive to follow a blameless course;
   oh, when will you come to me? *
      I will walk with sincerity of heart within my house.

3 I will set no worthless thing before my eyes; *
      I hate the doers of evil deeds;
      they shall not remain with me.

4 A crooked heart shall be far from me; *
      I will not know evil.

5 Those who in secret slander their neighbors I will destroy; *
      those who have a haughty look and a proud
         heart I cannot abide.

6 My eyes are upon the faithful in the land, that they may
         dwell with me, *
      and only those who lead a blameless life shall
         be my servants.

7 Those who act deceitfully shall not dwell in my house, *
      and those who tell lies shall not continue in my sight.

8 I will soon destroy all the wicked in the land, *
      that I may root out all evildoers from the city of God.

Twentieth Day: Morning Prayer

Psalm 102

1 O God, hear my prayer, and let my cry come before you; *
      hide not your face from me in the day of my trouble.

2 Incline your ear to me; *
      when I call, make haste to answer me,

3 For my days drift away like smoke, *
   and my bones are hot as burning coals.

4 My heart is smitten like grass and withered, *
   so that I forget to eat my bread.

5 Because of the voice of my groaning, *
   I am but skin and bones.

6 I have become like a vulture in the wilderness, *
   like an owl among the ruins.

7 I lie awake and groan; *
   I am like a sparrow, lonely on a house-top.

8 My enemies revile me all day long, *
   and those who scoff at me have taken an oath against me.

9 For I have eaten ashes for bread *
   and mingled my drink with weeping.

10 Because of your indignation and wrath, *
   you have lifted me up and thrown me away.

11 My days pass away like a shadow, *
   and I wither like the grass.

12 But you, O God, endure for ever, *
   and your Name from age to age.

13 You will arise and have compassion on Zion,
   for it is time to have mercy; *
   indeed, the appointed time has come.

14 For your servants love its very rubble *
   and are moved to pity even for its dust.

15 The nations shall fear your Name, O God, *
   and all the rulers of the earth your glory.

16 You, O God, will build up Zion, *
   and your glory will appear.

17 You will look with favor on the prayer of the homeless *
   and will not despise their plea.

18 Let this be written for a future generation, *
   so that a people yet unborn may praise you, O God.

19 For you looked down from your holy place on high; *
   from the heavens you beheld the earth,

20 That you might hear the groan of the captive *
   and set free those condemned to die,

21 That they may declare in Zion your Name, O God, *
   and your praise in Jerusalem,

22 When the peoples are gathered together, *
   and the nations also, to serve you.

23 You have brought down my strength before my time; *
   you have shortened the number of my days.

24 And I said, "O my God,
   do not take me away in the midst of my days; *
   your years endure throughout all generations.

25 In the beginning, O God, you laid the foundations
      of the earth, *
   and the heavens are the work of your hands.

26 They shall perish, but you will endure;
    they all shall wear out like a garment; *
        as clothing you will change them,
        and they shall be changed,

27 But you are always the same, *
    and your years will never end.

28 The children of your servants shall continue, *
    and their offspring shall stand fast in your sight."

Psalm 103

1 Bless the Holy One, O my soul, *
    and all that is within me, bless God's holy Name.

2 Bless the Holy One, O my soul, *
    and forget not all the gifts of God.

3 O God, you forgive all our sins, *
    and you heal all our infirmities;

4 You redeem our life from the grave *
    and crown us with mercy and loving-kindness;

5 You satisfy us with good things, *
    and our youth is renewed like an eagle's.

6 O God, you execute righteousness *
    and judgment for all who are oppressed.

7 You made your ways known to Moses *
    and your works to the children of Israel.

8 You are full of compassion and mercy, *
    slow to anger and of great kindness.

9 You will not always accuse us, *
    nor will you keep your anger for ever.

10 You have not dealt with us according to our sins, *
    nor rewarded us according to our wickedness.

11 For as the heavens are high above the earth, *
    so is your mercy great upon those who fear you.

12 As far as the east is from the west, *
    so far have you removed our sins from us.

13 As a parent cares for a child, *
    so do you care for those who fear you.

14 For you yourself know whereof we are made; *
    you remember that we are but dust.

15 Our days are like the grass; *
    we flourish like a flower of the field;

16 When the wind goes over it, it is gone, *
    and its place shall know it no more.

17 But your merciful goodness endures for ever
        on those who fear you, *
    and your righteousness on children's children;

18 On those who keep your covenant *
    and remember your commandments and do them.

19 You have set your throne in heaven, *
    and you have dominion over all.

20 Bless God, all you angels,
    you mighty ones who do God's bidding, *
    and hearken to the voice of God's word.

21 Bless God, all you heavenly hosts, *
    you ministers who do God's will.

22 Bless God, all creation,
    in all places of God's dominion; *
    bless the Holy One, O my soul.

Twentieth Day: Evening Prayer

Psalm 104

1 Bless the Holy One, O my soul; *
    O God, how excellent is your greatness;
    you are clothed with majesty and splendor.

2 You wrap yourself with light as with a cloak; *
    you spread out the heavens like a curtain.

3 You lay the beams of your chambers in the waters above; *
    you make the clouds your chariot;
    you ride on the wings of the wind.

4 You make the winds your messengers *
    and flames of fire your servants.

5 You have set the earth upon its foundations, *
    so that it never shall move at any time.

6 You covered it with the Deep as with a mantle; *
    the waters stood higher than the mountains.

7 At your rebuke they fled; *
    at the voice of your thunder they hastened away.

8 They went up into the hills and down to
      the valleys beneath, *
  to the places you had appointed for them.

9 You set the limits that they should not pass; *
  they shall not again cover the earth.

10 You send the springs into the valleys; *
  they flow between the mountains.

11 All the beasts of the field drink their fill from them, *
  and the wild asses quench their thirst.

12 Beside them the birds of the air make their nests *
  and sing among the branches.

13 You water the mountains from your dwelling on high; *
  the earth is fully satisfied by the fruit of your works.

14 You make grass grow for flocks and herds *
  and plants to serve all people;

15 That they may bring forth food from the earth, *
  and wine to gladden our hearts,

16 Oil to make a cheerful countenance, *
  and bread to strengthen the heart.

17 The trees of the Holy One are full of sap, *
  the cedars of Lebanon which God planted,

18 In which the birds build their nests, *
  and in whose tops the storks make their dwellings.

19 The high hills are a refuge for the mountain goats,*
  and the stony cliffs for the rock badgers.

20 You appointed the moon to mark the seasons,*
    and the sun knows the time of its setting.

21 You make darkness that it may be night,*
    in which all the beasts of the forest prowl.

22 The lions roar after their prey *
    and seek their food from God.

23 The sun rises, and they slip away *
    and lay themselves down in their dens.

24 We go forth to our work*
    and to our labor until the evening.

25 O Holy One, how manifold are your works;*
    in wisdom you have made them all;
    the earth is full of your creatures.

26 Yonder is the great and wide sea
  with its living things too many to number,*
    creatures both small and great.

27 There move the ships,
  and there is that Leviathan, *
    which you have made for the sport of it.

28 All of them look to you *
    to give them their food in due season.

29 You give it to them; they gather it; *
    you open your hand, and they are filled with good things.

30 You hide your face, and they are terrified; *
    you take away their breath,
    and they die and return to their dust.

31 You send forth your Spirit, and they are created; *
   and so you renew the face of the earth.

32 May the glory of God endure for ever; *
   may the Holy One rejoice in all creation.

33 God looks at the earth and it trembles; *
   God touches the mountains and they smoke.

34 I will sing to God as long as I live; *
   I will praise my God while I have my being.

35 May these words of mine find favor; *
   I will rejoice in the Holy One.

36 Let sinners be consumed out of the earth, *
   and the wicked be no more.

37 Bless the Holy One, O my soul. *
   Alleluia!

Twenty-first Day: Morning Prayer

Psalm 105

Part I

1 We give you thanks, O God, and call upon your Name; *
  we make known your deeds among the peoples.

2 We sing to you; we sing your praise *
  and speak of all your marvelous works.

3 We glory in your holy Name; *
  let the hearts of those who seek you rejoice.

4 We search for you and your strength; *
  we continue to seek your face.

5 We remember the marvels you have done, *
  the wonders and the judgments of your mouth,

6 We, the offspring of Abraham, your servant, *
  we, the children of Jacob, the chosen ones.

7 You are our God indeed; *
  your judgments prevail in all the world.

8 You have always been mindful of your covenant, *
  the promise you made for a thousand generations:

9 The covenant you made with Abraham, *
  the oath that you swore to Isaac,

10 Which you established as a statute for Jacob, *
  an everlasting covenant for Israel,

11 Saying, "To them will I give the land of Canaan *
  to be their allotted inheritance."

12 When they were few in number, *
  of little account, and sojourners in the land,

13 Wandering from nation to nation *
  and from one realm to another,

14 You let no one oppress them *
  and rebuked monarchs for their sake,

15 Saying, "Do not touch my anointed *
  and do my prophets no harm."

16 Then you called for a famine in the land *
   and destroyed the supply of bread.

17 You sent a man before them, *
   Joseph, who was sold as a slave.

18 They bruised his feet in fetters; *
   his neck they put in an iron collar.

19 Until his prediction came to pass, *
   your word, O Most High, tested him.

20 The king sent and released him; *
   the ruler of the peoples set him free.

21 He set him as a master over his household, *
   as a ruler over all his possessions,

22 To instruct his princes according to his will *
   and to teach his elders wisdom.

PSALM 105: PART II

23 Israel came into Egypt, *
   and Jacob became a sojourner in the land of Ham.

24 You made your people exceedingly fruitful; *
   you made them stronger than their enemies,

25 Whose hearts you turned, so that they hated your people *
   and dealt unjustly with your servants.

26 You sent Moses your servant, *
   and Aaron whom you had chosen.

27 They worked your signs among them, *
   and portents in the land of Ham.

28 You sent darkness, and it grew dark; *
    but the Egyptians rebelled against your words.

29 You turned their waters into blood *
    and caused their fish to die.

30 Their land was overrun by frogs, *
    in the very chambers of their rulers.

31 You spoke, and there came swarms of insects *
    and gnats within all their borders.

32 You gave them hailstones instead of rain, *
    and flames of fire throughout their land.

33 You blasted their vines and their fig trees *
    and shattered every tree in their country.

34 You spoke, and the locust came, *
    and young locusts without number,

35 Which ate up all the green plants in their land *
    and devoured the fruit of their soil.

36 You struck down the firstborn of their land, *
    the firstfruits of all their strength.

37 You led out your people with silver and gold; *
    in all their tribes there was not one that stumbled.

38 Egypt was glad of their going, *
    because they were afraid of them.

39 You spread out a cloud for a covering *
    and a fire to give light in the night season.

40 They asked, and quails appeared, *
   and you satisfied them with bread from heaven.

41 You opened the rock, and water flowed, *
   so the river ran in the dry places.

42 For you remembered your holy word *
   and Abraham your servant.

43 So you led forth your people with gladness, *
   your chosen with shouts of joy.

44 You gave your people the lands of the nations, *
   and they took the fruit of others' toil,

45 That they might keep your statutes *
   and observe your laws. Alleluia!

Twenty-first Day: Evening Prayer

Psalm 106

Part I

1 Alleluia! Give thanks, for the Holy One is good; *
   God's mercy endures for ever.

2 Who can declare the mighty acts of God *
   or show forth rightful praise?

3 Happy are they who act with justice *
   and always do what is right!

4 Remember me, O God, with the favor you have
          for your people, *
   and visit me with your saving help,

5 That I may see the prosperity of your elect
  and be glad with the gladness of your people; *
    that I may glory with your inheritance.

6 We have sinned as our forebears did; *
    we have done wrong and dealt wickedly.

7 In Egypt they did not consider your marvelous works
  nor remember the abundance of your love; *
    they defied you, O Most High, at the Red Sea.

8 But you saved them for your Name's sake, *
    to make your power known.

9 You rebuked the Red Sea, and it dried up, *
    and you led them through the deep as through a desert.

10 You saved them from the hand of those who hated them *
    and redeemed them from the hand of the enemy.

11 The waters covered their oppressors; *
    not one of them was left.

12 Then they believed your words *
    and sang you songs of praise.

13 But they soon forgot your deeds *
    and did not wait for your counsel.

14 A craving seized them in the wilderness, *
    and they put you to the test in the desert.

15 You gave them what they asked, *
    but sent leanness into their soul.

16 They envied Moses in the camp, *
    and Aaron, the holy one of God.

17 The earth opened and swallowed Dathan *
    and covered the company of Abiram.

18 Fire blazed up against their company, *
    and flames devoured the wicked.

PSALM 106: PART II

19 Israel made a bull-calf at Horeb *
    and worshiped a molten image;

20 And so they exchanged their Glory *
    for the image of an ox that feeds on grass.

21 They forgot you, their Savior, *
    who had done great things in Egypt,

22 Wonderful deeds in the land of Ham, *
    and fearful things at the Red Sea.

23 So you would have destroyed them,
    had not Moses your chosen stood before you in the breach, *
    to turn away your wrath from consuming them.

24 They refused the pleasant land *
    and would not believe your promise.

25 They grumbled in their tents *
    and would not listen to your voice, O God.

26 So you lifted your hand against them, *
    to overthrow them in the wilderness,

27 To cast out their seed among the nations, *
    and to scatter them throughout the lands.

28 They joined themselves to Baal-Peor *
    and ate sacrifices offered to the dead.

29 They provoked you to anger with their actions, *
    and a plague broke out among them.

30 Then Phinehas stood up and interceded, *
    and the plague came to an end.

31 This was reckoned to him as righteousness *
    throughout all generations for ever.

32 Again they provoked your anger at the waters of Meribah, *
    so that you punished Moses because of them;

33 For they so embittered his spirit *
    that he spoke rash words with his lips.

34 They did not destroy the peoples *
    as you had commanded them.

35 They intermingled with the nations *
    and learned their foreign ways,

36 So that they worshiped their idols, *
    which became a snare to them.

37 They sacrificed their sons *
    and their daughters to evil spirits.

38 They shed innocent blood,
the blood of their sons and daughters, *
    which they offered to the idols of Canaan,
    and the land was defiled with blood.

39 Thus they were polluted by their actions *
    and went whoring in their evil deeds.

40 Therefore your wrath was kindled against your people, *
    and you abhorred your inheritance.

41 You gave them over to the hand of the nations, *
    and those who hated them ruled over them.

42 Their enemies oppressed them, *
    and they were humbled under their hand.

43 Many a time did you deliver them,
    but they rebelled through their own devices *
    and were brought down in their iniquity.

44 Nevertheless, you saw their distress, *
    when you heard their lamentation.

45 You remembered your covenant with them *
    and relented in accordance with your great mercy.

46 You caused them to be pitied *
    by those who held them captive.

47 Save us, O God,
    and gather us from among the nations, *
    that we may give thanks to your holy Name
    and glory in your praise.

48 Blest be the God of Israel,
    from everlasting and to everlasting, *
    and let all the people say, "Amen!" Alleluia!

BOOK FIVE

Twenty-second Day: Morning Prayer

PSALM 107

PART I

1 We give you thanks, O God, for you are good; *
 your mercy endures for ever.

2 Let all those whom you have redeemed proclaim *
 that you redeemed them from the hand of the foe.

3 You gathered them out of the lands, *
 from the east and from the west,
 from the north and from the south.

4 Some wandered in desert wastes; *
 they found no way to a city where they might dwell.

5 They were hungry and thirsty; *
 their spirits languished within them.

6 Then they cried to you in their trouble, *
 and you delivered them from their distress.

7 You put their feet on a straight path *
 to go to a city where they might dwell.

8 Let them give thanks to you for your mercy *
 and the wonders you do for your children.

9 For you satisfy the thirsty *
 and fill the hungry with good things.

10 Some sat in darkness and deep gloom, *
     bound fast in misery and iron,

11 Because they rebelled against your words, O God, *
     and despised your counsel, O Most High.

12 So you humbled their spirits with hard labor; *
     they stumbled, and there was none to help.

13 Then they cried to you in their trouble, *
     and you delivered them from their distress.

14 You led them out of darkness and deep gloom, *
     and broke their bonds asunder.

15 Let them give thanks to you for your mercy *
     and the wonders you do for your children,

16 For you shatter the doors of bronze *
     and break in two the iron bars.

17 Some were fools and took to rebellious ways; *
     they were afflicted because of their sins.

18 They abhorred all manner of food *
     and drew near to death's door.

19 Then they cried to you in their trouble, *
     and you delivered them from their distress.

20 You sent forth your word and healed them, *
     and saved them from the grave.

21 Let them give thanks to you for your mercy *
     and the wonders you do for your children.

22 Let them offer a sacrifice of thanksgiving, *
     and tell of your acts with shouts of joy.

23 Some went down to the sea in ships *
    and plied their trade in deep waters;

24 They beheld your works, O God, *
    and your wonders in the deep.

25 Then you spoke, and a stormy wind arose, *
    which tossed high the waves of the sea.

26 They mounted up to the heavens and fell back to the depths; *
    their hearts melted because of their peril.

27 They reeled and staggered like drunkards *
    and were at their wits' end.

28 Then they cried to you in their trouble, *
    and you delivered them from their distress.

29 You stilled the storm to a whisper *
    and quieted the waves of the sea.

30 Then were they glad because of the calm, *
    and you brought them to the harbor they were bound for.

31 Let them give thanks to you for your mercy *
    and the wonders you do for your children.

32 Let them exalt you in the congregation of the people *
    and praise you in the council of the elders.

PSALM 107: PART II

33 You changed rivers into deserts *
    and water-springs into thirsty ground,

34 A fruitful land into salt flats, *
    because of the wickedness of those who dwell there.

35 You changed deserts into pools of water *
   and dry land into water-springs.

36 You settled the hungry there, *
   and they founded a city to dwell in.

37 They sowed fields and planted vineyards, *
   and brought in a fruitful harvest.

38 You blessed them, so that they increased greatly; *
   you did not let their herds decrease.

39 Yet when they were diminished and brought low *
   through stress of adversity and sorrow,

40 (You pour contempt on princes *
   and make them wander in trackless wastes),

41 You lifted up the poor out of misery *
   and multiplied their families like flocks of sheep.

42 The upright will see this and rejoice, *
   but all wickedness will shut its mouth.

43 Whoever is wise will ponder these things *
   and consider well your mercies, O God.

Twenty-second Day: Evening Prayer

PSALM 108

1 My heart is firmly fixed, O God, my heart is fixed; *
   I will sing and make melody.

2 Wake up, my spirit;
  awake, lute and harp; *
    I myself will waken the dawn.

3 I will confess you among the peoples, O God; *
    I will sing praises to you among the nations.

4 For your loving-kindness is greater than the heavens, *
    and your faithfulness reaches to the clouds.

5 Exalt yourself above the heavens, O God, *
    and your glory over all the earth.

6 So that those who are dear to you may be delivered, *
    save with your right hand and answer me.

7 God spoke from the holy place and said: *
    "I will exult and parcel out Shechem;
    I will divide the valley of Succoth.

8 Gilead is mine and Manasseh is mine; *
    Ephraim is my helmet and Judah my scepter.

9 Moab is my wash-basin;
  on Edom I throw down my sandal to claim it, *
    and over Philistia will I shout in triumph."

10 Who will lead me into the strong city; *
    who will bring me into Edom?

11 Have you not cast us off, O God? *
    You no longer go out, O God, with our armies.

12 Grant us your help against the enemy, *
    for all human help is in vain.

13 With you, O God, we will do valiant deeds, *
    and you will tread our enemies under foot.

Psalm 109

1 Hold not your tongue, O God of my praise, *
    for the mouth of the wicked,
    the mouth of the deceitful, is opened against me.

2 They speak to me with a lying tongue; *
    they encompass me with hateful words
    and fight against me without a cause.

3 Despite my love, they accuse me, *
    but as for me, I pray for them.

4 They repay evil for good *
    and hatred for my love.

5 Set wicked ones against them, *
    and let accusers stand at their right hand.

6 When they are judged, let them be found guilty, *
    and let their appeals be in vain.

7 Let their days be few, *
    and let others take their office.

8 Let their children be fatherless *
    and their wives become widows.

9 Let their children be waifs and beggars; *
    let them be driven from the ruins of their homes.

10 Let the creditor seize everything they have; *
    let strangers plunder their gains.

11 Let there be no one to show them kindness, *
   and none to pity their fatherless children.

12 Let their descendants be destroyed, *
   and their names be blotted out in the next generation.

13 Let the wickedness of their parents be remembered
           before God, *
   and their forebears' sin not be blotted out;

14 Let their sin be always before God, *
   but let God root out their names from the earth;

15 Because they did not remember to show mercy, *
   but persecuted the poor and needy
   and sought to kill the brokenhearted.

16 They loved cursing,
   let it come upon them; *
   they took no delight in blessing,
   let it depart from them.

17 They put on cursing like a garment; *
   let it soak into their bodies like water
   and into their bones like oil;

18 Let it be to them like the cloak which they wrap
           around themselves *
   and like the belt that they wear continually.

19 Let this be the recompense from God to my accusers *
   and to those who speak evil against me.

20 But you, O God, my God,
   oh, deal with me according to your Name; *
   for your tender mercy's sake, deliver me.

21 For I am poor and needy, *
     and my heart is wounded within me.

22 I have faded away like a shadow when it lengthens; *
     I am shaken off like a locust.

23 My knees are weak through fasting, *
     and my flesh is wasted and gaunt.

24 I have become a reproach to them; *
     they see and shake their heads.

25 Help me, O God, my God; *
     save me for your mercy's sake.

26 Let them know that this is your hand, *
     that you, O God, have done it.

27 They may curse, but you will bless; *
     let those who rise up against me be put to shame,
     and your servant will rejoice.

28 Let my accusers be clothed with disgrace *
     and wrap themselves in their shame as in a cloak.

29 I will give great thanks to you with my mouth; *
     in the midst of the multitude will I praise you,

30 Because you stand at the right hand of the needy, *
     to save their lives from those who would condemn them.

PSALM 110

1 The Holy One said to my Ruler, "Sit at my right hand, *
    until I make your enemies your footstool."

2 The Holy One will send the scepter of your power
        out of Zion, *
    saying, "Rule over your enemies round about you.

3 Royal state has been yours from the day of your birth; *
    in the beauty of holiness have I begotten you,
    like dew from the womb of the morning."

4 The Holy One has sworn and will not recant: *
    "You are a priest for ever after the order of Melchizedek."

5 The Ruler who is at your right hand
    will smite monarchs in the day of wrath *
    and will rule over the nations;

6 Will heap high the corpses, *
    and will smash heads over the wide earth.

7 The Ruler will drink from the brook beside the road, *
    and therefore will stand victorious.

PSALM 111

1 Alleluia! I will give thanks to you, O God, with
        my whole heart, *
    in the assembly of the upright, in the congregation.

2 Great are your deeds, O God; *
    they are studied by all who delight in them.

3 Your work is full of majesty and splendor, *
   and your righteousness endures for ever.

4 You make your marvelous works to be remembered; *
   you are gracious and full of compassion.

5 You give food to those who fear you; *
   you are ever mindful of your covenant.

6 You have shown your people the power of your works *
   in giving them the lands of the nations.

7 The works of your hands are faithfulness and justice; *
   all your commandments are sure.

8 They stand fast for ever and ever, *
   because they are done in truth and equity.

9 You sent redemption to your people;
   you commanded your covenant for ever; *
   holy and awesome is your Name.

10 The fear of God is the beginning of wisdom; *
   those who act accordingly have a good understanding;
   God's praise endures for ever.

PSALM 112

1 Alleluia! Happy are they who fear God *
   and have great delight in the commandments!

2 Their descendants will be mighty in the land; *
   the generation of the upright will be blest.

3 Wealth and riches will be in their house, *
   and their righteousness will last for ever.

4 Light shines in the darkness for the upright; *
   the righteous are merciful and full of compassion.

5 It is good for them to be generous in lending *
   and to manage their affairs with justice.

6 For they will never be shaken; *
   the righteous will be kept in everlasting remembrance.

7 They will not be afraid of any evil rumors; *
   their heart is right;
   they put their trust in God.

8 Their heart is established and will not shrink, *
   until they see their desire upon their enemies.

9 They have given freely to the poor, *
   and their righteousness stands fast for ever;
   they will hold up their head with honor.

10 The wicked will see it and be angry;
   they will gnash their teeth and pine away; *
   the desires of the wicked will perish.

PSALM 113

1 Alleluia! Give praise, you servants of God; *
   praise the Name of the Most High.

2 Let God's Name be blest, *
   from this time forth for evermore.

3 From the rising of the sun to its going down, *
   let God's holy Name be praised.

4 God is high above all nations, *
   and God's glory above the heavens.

5 Who is like our God, who sits enthroned on high, *
   but stoops to behold the heavens and the earth?

6 God takes up the weak out of the dust *
   and lifts up the poor from the ashes,

7 To set them up on high, *
   with the rulers of the people.

8 God makes the woman of a childless house *
   to be a joyful mother of children.

Twenty-third Day: Evening Prayer

Psalm 114

1 Alleluia! When Israel came out of Egypt, *
   the house of Jacob from a people of strange speech,

2 Judah became God's sanctuary *
   and Israel God's dominion.

3 The sea beheld it and fled; *
   Jordan turned and went back.

4 The mountains skipped like rams, *
   and the little hills like young sheep.

5 What ailed you, O sea, that you fled; *
   O Jordan, that you turned back?

6 You mountains, that you skipped like rams; *
   you little hills, like young sheep?

7 Tremble, O earth, at the presence of God, *
   at the presence of the God of Jacob,

8 Who turned the hard rock into a pool of water *
   and flint-stone into a flowing spring.

Psalm 115

1 Not to us, O God, not to us,
   but to your Name give glory, *
      because of your love and because of your faithfulness.

2 Why should the nations say, *
   "Where then is their God?"

3 Our God is in heaven, *
   and whatever God wills to do comes to pass.

4 Their idols are silver and gold, *
   the work of human hands.

5 They have mouths, but they cannot speak; *
   eyes have they, but they cannot see;

6 They have ears, but they cannot hear; *
   noses, but they cannot smell;

7 They have hands, but they cannot feel;
   feet, but they cannot walk; *
      they make no sound with their throat.

8 Those who make them are like them, *
   and so are all who put their trust in them.

9 O Israel, trust in God, *
   who is their help and their shield.

10 O house of Aaron, trust in God, *
     who is their help and their shield.

11 You who fear God, trust in God, *
     who is their help and their shield.

12 God has been mindful of us and will bless us; *
     God will bless the house of Israel
     and will bless the house of Aaron;

13 God will bless those who stand in awe, *
     both small and great together.

14 May God increase you more and more, *
     you and your children after you.

15 May you be blessed by God, *
     the maker of heaven and earth.

16 The heaven of heavens belongs to God, *
     who entrusted the earth to its peoples.

17 The dead do not praise God, *
     nor all those who go down into silence;

18 But we will bless God, *
     from this time forth for evermore. Alleluia!

Twenty-fourth Day: Morning Prayer

PSALM 116

1 I love you, O God, because you have heard the voice
     of my supplication, *
     because you have inclined your ear to me whenever
     I called upon you.

2 The cords of death entangled me;
   the grip of the grave took hold of me; *
      I came to grief and sorrow.

3 Then I called upon your holy Name: *
      "O God, I pray you, save my life."

4 Gracious are you and righteous; *
      you are full of compassion.

5 You watch over the innocent; *
      I was brought very low, and you helped me.

6 Turn again to your rest, O my soul, *
      for God has treated you well.

7 For you, O God, have rescued my life from death, *
      my eyes from tears, and my feet from stumbling.

8 I will walk in the presence of God, *
      in the land of the living.

9 I believed, even when I said,
   "I have been brought very low." *
      In my distress I said, "No one can be trusted."

10 How shall I repay God *
      for all the good things done for me?

11 I will lift up the cup of salvation *
      and call upon the Name of God.

12 I will fulfill my vows to God *
      in the presence of all people.

13 Precious in your sight, O God, *
      is the death of your servants.

14 O God, I am your servant; *
   I am your servant and the child of your handmaid;
   you have freed me from my bonds.

15 I will offer you the sacrifice of thanksgiving *
   and call upon your holy Name.

16 I will fulfill my vows to you *
   in the presence of all your people,

17 In the courts of God's house, *
   in the midst of you, O Jerusalem. Alleluia!

PSALM 117

1 Praise God, all you nations; *
   laud the Most High, all you peoples.

2 For God's loving-kindness toward us is great, *
   and the faithfulness of God endures for ever. Alleluia!

PSALM 118

1 Give thanks to God who is good; *
   God's mercy endures for ever.

2 Let Israel now proclaim: *
   "God's mercy endures for ever."

3 Let the house of Aaron now proclaim: *
   "God's mercy endures for ever."

4 Let those who fear God now proclaim: *
   "God's mercy endures for ever."

5 I called out in my distress; *
    God answered by setting me free.

6 The Mighty One is at my side, therefore I will not fear; *
    what can anyone do to me?

7 God is at my side to help me; *
    I will triumph over those who hate me.

8 It is better to rely on God *
    than to put any trust in flesh.

9 It is better to rely on God *
    than to put any trust in rulers.

10 All the ungodly encompass me; *
    in the name of God I will repel them.

11 They hem me in, they hem me in on every side; *
    in the name of God I will repel them.

12 They swarm about me like bees;
   they blaze like a fire of thorns; *
    in the name of God I will repel them.

13 I was pressed so hard that I almost fell, *
    but God came to my help.

14 God is my strength and my song *
    and has become my salvation.

15 There is a sound of exultation and victory *
    in the tents of the righteous:

16 "The right hand of the Most High has triumphed; *
    the right hand of the Most High is exalted;
    the right hand of the Most High has triumphed!"

17 I shall not die, but live *
 and declare the works of God.

18 God has punished me sorely, *
 but did not hand me over to death.

19 Open for me the gates of righteousness; *
 I will enter them;
 I will offer thanks to God.

20 "This is the gate of the Holy One; *
 those who are righteous may enter."

21 I will give thanks to you, for you answered me *
 and have become my salvation.

22 The same stone which the builders rejected *
 has become the chief cornerstone.

23 This is God's doing, *
 and it is marvelous in our eyes.

24 On this day the Holy One has acted; *
 we will rejoice and be glad in it.

25 Hosanna, O God, hosanna! *
 O Holy One, send us now success.

26 Blest is the one who comes in the name of God; *
 we bless you from the house of God.

27 God is the Holy One who has shined upon us; *
 form a procession with branches up to
 the horns of the altar.

28 "You are my God, and I will thank you; *
 you are my God, and I will exalt you."

29 Give thanks to God who is good; *
    God's mercy endures for ever.

Twenty-fourth Day: Evening Prayer

PSALM 119:1-32

ALEPH

1 Happy are they whose way is blameless, *
    who walk in your law, O God!

2 Happy are they who observe your decrees *
    and seek you with all their hearts;

3 Who never do any wrong, *
    but always walk in your ways.

4 You laid down your commandments, *
    that we should fully keep them.

5 Oh, that my ways were made so direct *
    that I might keep your statutes!

6 Then I should not be put to shame *
    when I regard all your commandments.

7 I will thank you with an unfeigned heart *
    when I have learned your righteous judgments.

8 I will keep your statutes; *
    do not utterly forsake me.

BETH

9 How shall young ones cleanse their ways? *
   By keeping to your words.

10 With my whole heart I seek you; *
   let me not stray from your commandments.

11 I treasure your promise in my heart, *
   that I may not sin against you.

12 Blest are you, O God; *
   instruct me in your statutes.

13 With my lips will I recite *
   all the judgments of your mouth.

14 I have taken greater delight in the way of your decrees *
   than in all manner of riches.

15 I will meditate on your commandments *
   and give attention to your ways.

16 My delight is in your statutes; *
   I will not forget your word.

GIMEL

17 Deal bountifully with your servant, *
   that I may live and keep your word.

18 Open my eyes, that I may see *
   the wonders of your law.

19 I am a stranger here on earth; *
   do not hide your commandments from me.

20 My soul is consumed at all times *
    with longing for your judgments.

21 You have rebuked the insolent; *
    cursed are they who stray from your commandments!

22 Turn from me shame and rebuke, *
    for I have kept your decrees.

23 Even though rulers sit and plot against me, *
    I will meditate on your statutes.

24 For your decrees are my delight, *
    and they are my counselors.

DALETH

25 My soul cleaves to the dust; *
    give me life according to your word.

26 I have confessed my ways, and you answered me; *
    instruct me in your statutes.

27 Make me understand the way of your commandments, *
    that I may meditate on your marvelous works.

28 My soul melts away for sorrow; *
    strengthen me according to your word.

29 Take from me the way of lying; *
    let me find grace through your law.

30 I have chosen the way of faithfulness; *
    I have set your judgments before me.

31 I hold fast to your decrees; *
    O God, let me not be put to shame.

32 I will run the way of your commandments, *
    for you have set my heart at liberty.

Twenty-fifth Day: Morning Prayer

Psalm 119:33-72

He

33 Teach me, O God, the way of your statutes, *
    and I shall keep it to the end.

34 Give me understanding, and I shall keep your law; *
    I shall keep it with all my heart.

35 Make me go in the path of your commandments, *
    for that is my desire.

36 Incline my heart to your decrees *
    and not to unjust gain.

37 Turn my eyes from watching what is worthless; *
    give me life in your ways.

38 Fulfill your promise to your servant, *
    which you make to those who fear you.

39 Turn away the reproach which I dread, *
    because your judgments are good.

40 Behold, I long for your commandments; *
    in your righteousness preserve my life.

WAW

41 Let your loving-kindness come to me, O God, *
    and your salvation, according to your promise.

42 Then shall I have a word for those who taunt me, *
    because I trust in your words.

43 Do not take the word of truth out of my mouth, *
    for my hope is in your judgments.

44 I shall continue to keep your law; *
    I shall keep it for ever and ever.

45 I will walk at liberty, *
    because I study your commandments.

46 I will tell of your decrees before rulers *
    and will not be ashamed.

47 I delight in your commandments, *
    which I have always loved.

48 I will lift up my hands to your commandments, *
    and I will meditate on your statutes.

ZAYIN

49 Remember your word to your servant, *
    because you have given me hope.

50 This is my comfort in my trouble: *
    that your promise gives me life.

51 The proud have derided me cruelly, *
    but I have not turned from your law.

52 When I remember your judgments of old, *
    O God, I take great comfort.

53 I am filled with a burning rage, *
    because of the wicked who forsake your law.

54 Your statutes have been like songs to me *
    wherever I have lived as a stranger.

55 I remember your Name in the night, O God, *
    and dwell upon your law.

56 This is how it has been with me, *
    because I have kept your commandments.

HETH

57 You only are my portion, O God; *
    I have promised to keep your words.

58 I entreat you with all my heart: *
    be merciful to me according to your promise.

59 I have considered my ways *
    and turned my feet toward your decrees.

60 I hasten and do not tarry *
    to keep your commandments.

61 Though the cords of the wicked entangle me, *
    I do not forget your law.

62 At midnight I will rise to give you thanks, *
    because of your righteous judgments.

63 I am a companion of all who fear you *
    and of those who keep your commandments.

64 The earth, O God, is full of your love; *
    instruct me in your statutes.

TETH

65 O God, you have dealt graciously with your servant, *
    according to your word.

66 Teach me discernment and knowledge, *
    for I have believed in your commandments.

67 Before I was afflicted I went astray, *
    but now I keep your word.

68 You are good and you bring forth good; *
    instruct me in your statutes.

69 The proud have smeared me with lies, *
    but I will keep your commandments with my whole heart.

70 Their heart is gross and fat, *
    but my delight is in your law.

71 It is good for me that I have been afflicted, *
    that I might learn your statutes.

72 The law of your mouth is dearer to me *
    than thousands in gold and silver.

PSALM 119:73-104

YODH

73 Your hands have made me and fashioned me; *
 give me understanding, that I may learn your
  commandments.

74 Those who fear you will be glad when they see me, *
 because I trust in your word.

75 I know, O God, that your judgments are right, *
 and that in faithfulness you have afflicted me.

76 Let your loving-kindness be my comfort, *
 as you have promised to your servant.

77 Let your compassion come to me, that I may live, *
 for your law is my delight.

78 Let the arrogant be put to shame, for they wrong me
  with lies, *
 but I will meditate on your commandments.

79 Let those who fear you turn to me *
 and also those who know your decrees.

80 Let my heart be sound in your statutes, *
 that I may not be put to shame.

KAPH

81 My soul has longed for your salvation; *
 I have put my hope in your word.

82 My eyes have failed from watching for your promise, *
    and I say, "When will you comfort me?"

83 I have become like a leather flask in the smoke, *
    but I have not forgotten your statutes.

84 How much longer must I wait; *
    when will you give judgment against those who
        persecute me?

85 The proud have dug pits for me; *
    they do not keep your law.

86 All your commandments are true; *
    help me, for they persecute me with lies.

87 They had almost made an end of me on earth, *
    but I have not forsaken your commandments.

88 In your loving-kindness, revive me, *
    that I may keep the decrees of your mouth.

Lamedh

89 O God, your word is everlasting; *
    it stands firm in the heavens.

90 Your faithfulness remains from one generation to another; *
    you established the earth, and it abides.

91 By your decree these continue to this day, *
    for all things are your servants.

92 If my delight had not been in your law, *
    I should have perished in my affliction.

93 I will never forget your commandments, *
   because by them you give me life.

94 I am yours; oh, that you would save me, *
   for I study your commandments.

95 Though the wicked lie in wait for me to destroy me, *
   I will apply my mind to your decrees.

96 I see that all things come to an end, *
   but your commandment has no bounds.

MEM

97 Oh, how I love your law; *
   all the day long it is in my mind.

98 Your commandment has made me wiser than my enemies, *
   and it is always with me.

99 I have more understanding than all my teachers, *
   for your decrees are my study.

100 I am wiser than the elders, *
   because I observe your commandments.

101 I restrain my feet from every evil way, *
   that I may keep your word.

102 I do not shrink from your judgments, *
   because you yourself have taught me.

103 How sweet are your words to my taste; *
   they are sweeter than honey to my mouth.

104 Through your commandments I gain understanding; *
   therefore I hate every lying way.

PSALM 119:105-144

NUN

105 Your word is a lantern to my feet *
    and a light upon my path.

106 I have sworn and am determined *
    to keep your righteous judgments.

107 I am deeply troubled; *
    preserve my life, O God, according to your word.

108 Accept, O God, the willing tribute of my lips, *
    and teach me your judgments.

109 My life is always in my hand, *
    yet I do not forget your law.

110 The wicked have set a trap for me, *
    but I have not strayed from your commandments.

111 Your decrees are my inheritance for ever; *
    truly, they are the joy of my heart.

112 I have applied my heart to fulfill your statutes *
    for ever and to the end.

SAMEKH

113 I hate those who have a divided heart, *
    but your law do I love.

114 You are my refuge and shield; *
    my hope is in your word.

115 Away from me, you wicked! *
    I will keep the commandments of my God.

116 Sustain me according to your promise, that I may live, *
    and let me not be disappointed in my hope.

117 Hold me up, and I shall be safe, *
    and my delight shall be ever in your statutes.

118 You spurn all who stray from your statutes; *
    their deceitfulness is in vain.

119 In your sight all the wicked of the earth are but dross; *
    therefore I love your decrees.

120 My flesh trembles with dread of you; *
    I am afraid of your judgments.

AYIN

121 I have done what is just and right; *
    do not deliver me to my oppressors.

122 Be surety for your servant's good; *
    let not the proud oppress me.

123 My eyes have failed from watching for your salvation *
    and for your righteous promise.

124 Deal with your servant according to your loving-kindness, *
    and teach me your statutes.

125 I am your servant; grant me understanding, *
    that I may know your decrees.

126 It is time for you to act, O God, *
    for they have broken your law.

127 Truly, I love your commandments *
    more than gold and precious stones.

128 I hold all your commandments to be right for me; *
    all paths of falsehood I abhor.

Pᴇ

129 Your decrees are wonderful; *
    therefore I obey them with all my heart.

130 When your word goes forth it gives light; *
    it gives understanding to the simple.

131 I open my mouth and pant; *
    I long for your commandments.

132 Turn to me in mercy, *
    as you always do to those who love your Name.

133 Steady my footsteps in your word; *
    let no iniquity have dominion over me.

134 Rescue me from those who oppress me, *
    and I will keep your commandments.

135 Let your countenance shine upon your servant, *
    and teach me your statutes.

136 My eyes shed streams of tears, *
    because people do not keep your law.

Sᴀᴅʜᴇ

137 You are righteous, O God, *
    and upright are your judgments.

138 You have issued your decrees *
    with justice and in perfect faithfulness.

139 My indignation has consumed me, *
    because my enemies forget your words.

140 Your word has been tested to the uttermost, *
    and your servant holds it dear.

141 I am small and of little account, *
    yet I do not forget your commandments.

142 Your justice is an everlasting justice, *
    and your law is the truth.

143 Trouble and distress have come upon me, *
    yet your commandments are my delight.

144 The righteousness of your decrees is everlasting; *
    grant me understanding, that I may live.

Twenty-sixth Day: Evening Prayer

PSALM 119:145-176

QOPH

145 I call with my whole heart; *
    answer me, O God, that I may keep your statutes.

146 I call to you;
    oh, that you would save me! *
       I will keep your decrees.

147 Early in the morning I cry out to you, *
    for in your word is my trust.

148 My eyes are open in the night watches, *
    that I may meditate upon your promise.

149 Hear my voice, O God, according to your loving-kindness; *
    according to your judgments, give me life.

150 They draw near who in malice persecute me; *
    they are very far from your law.

151 You, O God, are near at hand, *
    and all your commandments are true.

152 Long have I known from your decrees *
    that you have established them for ever.

RESH

153 Behold my affliction and deliver me, *
    for I do not forget your law.

154 Plead my cause and redeem me; *
    according to your promise, give me life.

155 Deliverance is far from the wicked, *
    for they do not study your statutes.

156 Great is your compassion, O God; *
    preserve my life, according to your judgments.

157 There are many who persecute and oppress me, *
    yet I have not swerved from your decrees.

158 I look with loathing at the faithless, *
    for they have not kept your word.

159 See how I love your commandments! *
    O God, in your mercy, preserve me.

160 The heart of your word is truth; *
    all your righteous judgments endure for evermore.

SHIN

161 Rulers have persecuted me without a cause, *
    but my heart stands in awe of your word.

162 I am as glad because of your promise *
    as one who finds great spoils.

163 As for lies, I hate and abhor them, *
    but your law is my love.

164 Seven times a day do I praise you, *
    because of your righteous judgments.

165 Great peace have they who love your law; *
    for them there is no stumbling block.

166 I have hoped for your salvation, O God, *
    and I have fulfilled your commandments.

167 I have kept your decrees, *
    and I have loved them deeply.

168 I have kept your commandments and decrees, *
    for all my ways are before you.

TAW

169 Let my cry come before you, O God; *
    give me understanding, according to your word.

170 Let my supplication come before you; *
    deliver me, according to your promise.

171 My lips shall pour forth your praise, *
    when you teach me your statutes.

172 My tongue shall sing of your promise, *
    for all your commandments are righteous.

173 Let your hand be ready to help me, *
    for I have chosen your commandments.

174 I long for your salvation, O God, *
    and your law is my delight.

175 Let me live, and I will praise you, *
    and let your judgments help me.

176 I have gone astray like a sheep that is lost; *
    search for your servant,
    for I do not forget your commandments.

Twenty-seventh Day: Morning Prayer

PSALM 120

1 When I was in trouble, I called out to God; *
    I called out to God, who answered me.

2 Deliver me, O God, from lying lips *
    and from the deceitful tongue.

3 What shall be done to you, and what more besides, *
    O you deceitful tongue?

4 The sharpened arrows of a warrior, *
    along with hot glowing coals.

5 How hateful it is that I must lodge in Meshech *
    and dwell among the tents of Kedar!

6 Too long have I had to live *
    among the enemies of peace.

7 I am on the side of peace, *
    but when I speak of it, they are for war.

PSALM 121

1 I lift up my eyes to the hills; *
    from where is my help to come?

2 My help comes from God, *
    the maker of heaven and earth.

3 God will not let your foot be moved; *
    the One who watches over you will not fall asleep.

4 Behold, the One who keeps watch over Israel *
    shall neither slumber nor sleep;

5 The Holy One watches over you *
    and is your shade at your right hand,

6 So that the sun shall not strike you by day, *
    nor the moon by night.

7 God shall preserve you from all evil, *
    and is the One who shall keep you safe.

8 God shall watch over your going out and your coming in, *
    from this time forth for evermore.

Psalm 122

1 I was glad when they said to me, *
   "Let us go to the house of God."

2 Now our feet are standing *
   within your gates, O Jerusalem.

3 Jerusalem is built as a city *
   that is at unity with itself;

4 To which the tribes go up,
   the tribes of the Holy One, *
      the assembly of Israel,
      to praise the Name of God.

5 For there are the thrones of judgment, *
   the thrones of the house of David.

6 Pray for the peace of Jerusalem: *
   "May they prosper who love you.

7 Peace be within your walls *
   and quietness within your towers.

8 For my kindred and companions' sake, *
   I pray for your prosperity.

9 Because of the house of the Holy One our God, *
   I will seek to do you good."

Psalm 123

1 To you I lift up my eyes, *
   to you enthroned in the heavens.

2 As the eyes of servants look to the hand of their masters, *
    and the eyes of a maid to the hand of her mistress,

3 So our eyes look to the Holy One our God, *
    until God shows us mercy.

4 Have mercy upon us, O God, have mercy, *
    for we have had more than enough of contempt,

5 Too much of the scorn of the indolent rich, *
    and of the derision of the proud.

PSALM 124

1 If God had not been on our side, *
    let Israel now say;

2 If God had not been on our side, *
    when enemies rose up against us,

3 Then would they have swallowed us up alive *
    in their fierce anger toward us;

4 Then would the waters have overwhelmed us *
    and the torrent gone over us;

5 Then would the raging waters *
    have gone right over us.

6 Blessed be God, *
    who has not given us over to be a prey for their teeth.

7 We have escaped like a bird from the snare of the fowler; *
    the snare is broken, and we have escaped.

8 Our help is in the Name of God, *
    the maker of heaven and earth.

Psalm 125

1 They who trust in God are like Mount Zion, *
    which cannot be moved, but stands fast for ever.

2 The hills stand about Jerusalem; *
    so does God stand round about the people,
    from this time forth for evermore.

3 The scepter of the wicked shall not hold sway over
        the land allotted to the just, *
    so that the just shall not put their hands to evil.

4 Show your goodness, O God, to those who are good *
    and to those who are true of heart.

5 As for those who turn aside to crooked ways,
    God will lead them away with the evildoers; *
    but peace be upon Israel.

Twenty-seventh Day: Evening Prayer

Psalm 126

1 When God restored the fortunes of Zion, *
    then were we like those who dream.

2 Then was our mouth filled with laughter, *
    and our tongue with shouts of joy.

3 Then they said among the nations, *
    "God has done great things for them."

4 God has done great things for us, *
    and we are glad indeed.

5 Restore our fortunes, O God, *
   like the watercourses of the Negev.

6 Those who sowed with tears *
   will reap with songs of joy.

7 Those who go out weeping, carrying the seed, *
   will come again with joy, shouldering their sheaves.

PSALM 127

1 Unless God builds the house, *
   their labor is in vain who build it.

2 Unless God watches over the city, *
   in vain the sentries keep their vigil.

3 It is in vain that you rise so early and go to bed so late; *
   vain, too, to eat the bread of toil,
   for God gives to the beloved sleep.

4 Children are a heritage from God, *
   and the fruit of the womb is a gift.

5 Like arrows in the hand of a warrior *
   are the children of one's youth.

6 Happy are they who have their quivers full of them; *
   they shall not be put to shame
   when they contend with their enemies in the gate.

PSALM 128

1 Happy are they all who fear God, *
   and who follow in God's ways!

2 You shall eat the fruit of your labor; *
  happiness and prosperity shall be yours.

3 Your wife shall be like a fruitful vine within your house, *
  your children like olive shoots round about your table.

4 They who fear God *
  shall thus indeed be blest.

5 May God bless you from Zion, *
  and may you see the prosperity of Jerusalem all the
    days of your life.

6 May you live to see your children's children; *
  may peace be upon Israel.

Psalm 129

1 "Greatly have they oppressed me since my youth," *
  let Israel now say;

2 "Greatly have they oppressed me since my youth, *
  but they have not prevailed against me."

3 They scored my back as with a ploughshare *
  and made their furrows long.

4 Our God, the Righteous One, *
  has cut the cords of the wicked.

5 Let them be put to shame and thrown back, *
  all those who are enemies of Zion.

6 Let them be like grass upon the housetops, *
  which withers before it can be plucked;

7 Which does not fill the hand of the reaper, *
   nor the bosom of one who binds the sheaves;

8 So that those who go by say not so much as,
   "May God prosper you. *
   We wish you well in the Name of our God."

PSALM 130

1 Out of the depths have I called to you;
   O God, hear my voice; *
   let your ears consider well the voice of my supplication.

2 If you were to note what is done amiss, *
   O God, who could stand?

3 For there is forgiveness with you; *
   therefore you shall be feared.

4 I wait for you, O God; my soul waits for you; *
   in your word is my hope.

5 My soul waits for you,
   more than sentries for the morning, *
   more than sentries for the morning.

6 O Israel, wait upon God, *
   for with God there is mercy.

7 With God there is plenteous redemption; *
   God shall redeem Israel from all their sins.

Psalm 131

1 O God, I am not proud; *
   I have no haughty looks.

2 I do not occupy myself with great matters, *
   or with things that are too hard for me.

3 But I still my soul and make it quiet,
   like a child upon its mother's breast; *
   my soul is quieted within me.

4 O Israel, wait upon God, *
   from this time forth for evermore.

Twenty-eighth Day: Morning Prayer

Psalm 132

1 O God, remember David *
   and all the hardships he endured;

2 How he swore an oath to God *
   and vowed a vow to the Mighty One of Jacob:

3 "I will not come under the roof of my house, *
   nor climb up into my bed;

4 I will not allow my eyes to sleep, *
   nor let my eyelids slumber;

5 Until I find a place for you, O God, *
   a dwelling for you, O Mighty One of Jacob."

6 "The ark! We heard it was in Ephrathah; *
   we found it in the fields of Jearim.

7 Let us go to God's dwelling place; *
    let us fall upon our knees before God's footstool."

8 Arise, O God, into your resting-place, *
    you and the ark of your strength.

9 Let your priests be clothed with righteousness; *
    let your faithful people sing with joy.

10 For your servant David's sake, *
    do not turn away the face of your Anointed.

11 You have sworn an oath to David; *
    in truth, you will not break it:

12 "A son, the fruit of your body, *
    will I set upon your throne.

13 If your children keep my covenant
    and my testimonies that I shall teach them, *
    their children will sit upon your throne for evermore.

14 For God has chosen Zion *
    and has desired it for a habitation:

15 "This shall be my resting-place for ever; *
    here will I dwell, for I delight in it.

16 I will surely bless its provisions, *
    and satisfy its poor with bread.

17 I will clothe its priests with salvation, *
    and its faithful people will rejoice and sing.

18 There will I make the horn of David flourish; *
    I have prepared a lamp for my Anointed.

19 As for his enemies, I will clothe them with shame; *
    but as for him, his crown will shine."

Psalm 133

1 Oh, how good and pleasant it is, *
    when kindred live together in unity!

2 It is like fine oil upon the head *
    that runs down upon the beard,

3 Upon the beard of Aaron, *
    and runs down upon the collar of his robe.

4 It is like the dew of Hermon *
    that falls upon the hills of Zion.

5 For there has God ordained the blessing: *
    life for evermore.

Psalm 134

1 Behold now, bless God, all you servants of God, *
    you that stand by night in the house of God.

2 Lift up your hands in the holy place and bless God; *
    God who made heaven and earth bless you out of Zion.

Psalm 135

1 Alleluia! Praise the Name of the Holy One; *
    give praise, you servants of the Most High.

2 You who stand in the house of the Holy One, *
    in the courts of the house of our God.

3 Praise God, for God is good; *
   sing praises to the holy Name, for it is lovely.

4 For you, O God, have chosen Jacob for yourself *
   and Israel for your own possession.

5 For I know that you are great, *
   that you are above all gods.

6 You do whatever pleases you, in heaven and on earth, *
   in the seas and all the deeps.

7 You bring up rain clouds from the ends of the earth; *
   you send out lightning with the rain;
   you bring the winds out of your storehouse.

8 It was you who struck down the firstborn of Egypt, *
   the firstborn of all creatures.

9 You sent signs and wonders into the midst of Egypt, *
   against Pharaoh and all his servants.

10 You overthrew many nations *
   and put mighty kings to death:

11 Sihon, king of the Amorites,
   and Og, the king of Bashan, *
   and all the kingdoms of Canaan.

12 You gave their land to be an inheritance, *
   an inheritance for Israel your people.

13 O God, your Name is everlasting; *
   your renown endures from age to age.

14 For you give your people justice *
   and show compassion to your servants.

15 The idols of the nations are silver and gold, *
   the work of human hands.

16 They have mouths, but they cannot speak; *
   eyes have they, but they cannot see.

17 They have ears, but they cannot hear; *
   neither is there any breath in their mouth.

18 Those who make them are like them, *
   and so are all who put their trust in them.

19 Bless God, O house of Israel; *
   O house of Aaron, bless God.

20 Bless God, O house of Levi; *
   you who fear God, bless God.

21 Blest be the Most High out of Zion, *
   who dwells in Jerusalem. Alleluia!

Twenty-eighth Day: Evening Prayer

PSALM 136

1 Give thanks to the Holy One who is good, *
   for God's mercy endures for ever.

2 Give thanks to the God of gods, *
   for God's mercy endures for ever.

3 Give thanks to the Ruler of rulers, *
   for God's mercy endures for ever;

4 Who only does great wonders, *
   for God's mercy endures for ever;

5 Who by wisdom made the heavens, *
  for God's mercy endures for ever;

6 Who spread out the earth upon the waters, *
  for God's mercy endures for ever;

7 Who created great lights, *
  for God's mercy endures for ever;

8 The sun to rule the day, *
  for God's mercy endures for ever;

9 The moon and the stars to govern the night, *
  for God's mercy endures for ever;

10 Who struck down the firstborn of Egypt, *
  for God's mercy endures for ever;

11 And brought out Israel from among them, *
  for God's mercy endures for ever;

12 With a mighty hand and a stretched-out arm, *
  for God's mercy endures for ever;

13 Who divided the Red Sea in two, *
  for God's mercy endures for ever;

14 And made Israel to pass through the midst of it, *
  for God's mercy endures for ever;

15 But swept Pharaoh and his army into the Red Sea, *
  for God's mercy endures for ever;

16 Who led the people through the wilderness, *
  for God's mercy endures for ever;

17 Who struck down great kings, *
    for God's mercy endures for ever;

18 And slew mighty kings, *
    for God's mercy endures for ever;

19 Sihon, king of the Amorites, *
    for God's mercy endures for ever;

20 And Og, the king of Bashan, *
    for God's mercy endures for ever;

21 And gave away their lands for an inheritance, *
    for God's mercy endures for ever;

22 An inheritance for Israel God's servant, *
    for God's mercy endures for ever;

23 Who remembered us in our low estate, *
    for God's mercy endures for ever;

24 And delivered us from our enemies, *
    for God's mercy endures for ever;

25 Who gives food to all creatures, *
    for God's mercy endures for ever.

26 Give thanks to the God of heaven, *
    for God's mercy endures for ever.

PSALM 137

1 By the waters of Babylon we sat down and wept *
    when we remembered you, O Zion.

2 As for our harps, we hung them up *
    on the trees in the midst of that land.

3 For those who led us away captive asked us for a song,
and our oppressors called for mirth: *
  "Sing us one of the songs of Zion."

4 How shall we sing God's holy song *
  upon a foreign soil?

5 If I forget you, O Jerusalem, *
  let my right hand forget its skill.

6 Let my tongue cleave to the roof of my mouth
if I do not remember you, *
  if I do not set Jerusalem above my highest joy.

7 Remember the day of Jerusalem, O God,
against the people of Edom, *
  who said, "Down with it! Down with it,
  even to the ground!"

8 O Offspring of Babylon, doomed to destruction, *
  happy the one who pays you back
  for what you have done to us!

9 Happy shall be the one who takes your little ones *
  and dashes them against the rock!

Psalm 138

1 I will give thanks to you, O God, with my whole heart; *
  before the gods I will sing your praise.

2 I will bow down toward your holy temple
and praise your Name, *
  because of your love and faithfulness;

3 For you have glorified your Name *
   and your word above all things.

4 When I called, you answered me; *
   you increased my strength within me.

5 All the rulers of the earth will praise you, O God, *
   when they have heard the words of your mouth.

6 They will sing of the ways of God, *
   that great is the glory of God.

7 Although on high, God cares for the lowly *
   and perceives the haughty from afar.

8 Though I walk in the midst of trouble, you keep me safe; *
   you stretch forth your hand against the fury of my enemies;
   your right hand shall save me.

9 You will make good your purpose for me; *
   O God, your love endures for ever;
   do not abandon the works of your hands.

Twenty-ninth Day: Morning Prayer

Psalm 139

1 O God, you have searched me out and known me; *
   you know my sitting down and my rising up;
   you discern my thoughts from afar.

2 You trace my journeys and my resting-places, *
   and are acquainted with all my ways.

3 Indeed, there is not a word on my lips, *
  but you, O God, know it altogether.

4 You press upon me behind and before, *
  and lay your hand upon me.

5 Such knowledge is too wonderful for me; *
  it is so high that I cannot attain to it.

6 Where can I go then from your Spirit; *
  where can I flee from your presence?

7 If I climb up to heaven, you are there; *
  if I make the grave my bed, you are there also.

8 If I take the wings of the morning *
  and dwell in the uttermost parts of the sea,

9 Even there your hand will lead me, *
  and your right hand hold me fast.

10 If I say, "Surely the darkness will cover me, *
  and the light around me turn to night,"

11 Darkness is not dark to you;
  the night is as bright as the day; *
  darkness and light to you are both alike.

12 For you yourself created my inmost parts; *
  you knit me together in my mother's womb.

13 I will thank you because I am marvelously made; *
  your works are wonderful, and I know it well.

14 My body was not hidden from you, *
  while I was being made in secret
  and woven in the depths of the earth.

15 Your eyes beheld my limbs, yet unfinished in the womb;
      all of them were written in your book; *
         they were fashioned day by day,
         when as yet there was none of them.

16 How deep I find your thoughts, O God; *
      how great is the sum of them!

17 If I were to count them, they would be more in number
            than the sand; *
      to count them all, my life span would need to
            be like yours.

18 Oh, that you would slay the wicked, O God! *
      You that thirst for blood, depart from me.

19 They speak despitefully against you; *
      your enemies take your Name in vain.

20 Do I not hate those, O God, who hate you; *
      and do I not loathe those who rise up against you?

21 I hate them with a perfect hatred; *
      they have become my own enemies.

22 Search me out, O God, and know my heart; *
      try me and know my restless thoughts.

23 Look well whether there be any wickedness in me, *
      and lead me in the way that is everlasting.

PSALM 140

1 Deliver me, O God, from evildoers; *
      protect me from the violent,

2 Who devise evil in their hearts *
    and stir up strife all day long.

3 They have sharpened their tongues like a serpent; *
    adder's poison is under their lips.

4 Keep me, O God, from the hands of the wicked; *
    protect me from the violent,
    who are determined to trip me up.

5 The proud have hidden a snare for me
    and stretched out a net of cords; *
    they have set traps for me along the path.

6 I have said to God, "You are my God; *
    listen to my supplication.

7 O God, the strength of my salvation, *
    you have covered my head in the day of battle.

8 Do not grant the desires of the wicked, O God,*
    nor let their evil plans prosper.

9 Let not those who surround me lift up their heads; *
    let the evil of their lips overwhelm them.

10 Let hot burning coals fall upon them; *
    let them be cast into the mire, never to rise up again."

11 A slanderer shall not be established on the earth, *
    and evil shall hunt down the lawless.

12 I know that God will maintain the cause of the poor *
    and render justice to the needy.

13 Surely, the righteous will give thanks to your Name, *
    and the upright shall continue in your sight.

PSALM 141

1 O God, I call to you; come to me quickly; *
   hear my voice when I cry to you.

2 Let my prayer be set forth in your sight as incense, *
   the lifting up of my hands as the evening sacrifice.

3 Set a watch before my mouth, O God,
   and guard the door of my lips; *
   let not my heart incline to any evil thing.

4 Let me not be occupied in wickedness with evildoers, *
   nor eat of their choice foods.

5 Let the righteous smite me in friendly rebuke;
   let not the oil of the unrighteous anoint my head, *
   for my prayer is continually against their wicked deeds.

6 Let their rulers be overthrown in stony places, *
   that they may know my words are true.

7 As when a ploughshare turns over the earth in furrows, *
   let their bones be scattered at the mouth of the grave.

8 But my eyes are turned to you, O God; *
   in you I take refuge;
   do not strip me of my life.

9 Protect me from the snare which they have laid for me *
   and from the traps of the evildoers.

10 Let the wicked fall into their own nets, *
   while I myself escape.

1 I cry to you, O God, with my voice; *
  to you I make loud supplication.

2 I pour out my complaint before you *
  and tell you all my trouble.

3 When my spirit languishes within me, you know my path; *
  in the way wherein I walk they have hidden a trap for me.

4 I look to my right hand and find no one who knows me; *
  I have no place to flee to, and no one cares for me.

5 I cry out to you, O God; *
  I say, "You are my refuge,
    my portion in the land of the living."

6 Listen to my cry for help, for I have been brought very low; *
  save me from those who pursue me,
    for they are too strong for me.

7 Bring me out of prison, that I may give
        thanks to your Name; *
  when you have dealt bountifully with me,
    the righteous will gather around me.

Psalm **143**

1 O God, hear my prayer,
  and in your faithfulness heed my supplications; *
    answer me in your righteousness.

2 Enter not into judgment with your servant, *
  for in your sight shall no one living be justified.

3 For my enemy has sought my life,
  has crushed me to the ground, *
    and has made me live in dark places like those who
        are long dead.

4 My spirit faints within me; *
  my heart within me is desolate.

5 I remember the time past;
  I muse upon all your deeds; *
    I consider the works of your hands.

6 I spread out my hands to you; *
  my soul gasps to you like a thirsty land.

7 O God, make haste to answer me; my spirit fails me; *
  do not hide your face from me,
  or I shall be like those who go down to the Pit.

8 Let me hear of your loving-kindness in the morning,
  for I put my trust in you; *
    show me the road that I must walk,
    for I lift up my soul to you.

9 Deliver me from my enemies, O God, *
  for I flee to you for refuge.

10 Teach me to do what pleases you, for you are my God; *
  let your good Spirit lead me on level ground.

11 Revive me, O God, for your Name's sake; *
  for your righteousness' sake, bring me out of trouble.

12 Of your goodness, destroy my enemies
  and bring all my foes to naught, *
    for truly I am your servant.

PSALM 143   233

PSALM 144

1 Blessed be my God, my rock, *
    who trains my hands to fight and my fingers to battle;

2 My help and my fortress, my stronghold and my deliverer, *
    my shield in whom I trust,
    who subdues the peoples under me.

3 O God, what are we that you should care for us, *
    mere mortals that you should think of us?

4 We are like a puff of wind; *
    our days are like a passing shadow.

5 Bow your heavens, O God, and come down; *
    touch the mountains, and they shall smoke.

6 Hurl the lightning and scatter them; *
    shoot out your arrows and rout them.

7 Stretch out your hand from on high; *
    rescue me and deliver me from the great waters,
    from the hand of foreign peoples,

8 Whose mouths speak deceitfully *
    and whose right hand is raised in falsehood.

9 O God, I will sing to you a new song; *
    I will play to you on a ten-stringed lyre.

10 You give victory to rulers *
    and have rescued David your servant.

11 Rescue me from the hurtful sword, *
    and deliver me from the hand of foreign peoples,

12 Whose mouths speak deceitfully *
    and whose right hand is raised in falsehood.

13 May our sons be like plants well nurtured from their youth, *
    and our daughters like sculptured corners of a palace.

14 May our barns be filled to overflowing with all manner
        of crops; *
    may the flocks in our pastures increase by thousands
        and tens of thousands;
    may our cattle be fat and sleek.

15 May there be no breaching of the walls, no going into exile, *
    no wailing in the public squares.

16 Happy are the people of whom this is so; *
    happy are the people who worship God!

PSALM 145

1 I will exalt you, O holy God, *
    and bless your Name for ever and ever.

2 Every day will I bless you *
    and praise your Name for ever and ever.

3 Great are you, O God, and greatly to be praised; *
    there is no end to your greatness.

4 One generation shall praise your works to another *
    and shall declare your power.

5 I will ponder the glorious splendor of your majesty *
   and all your marvelous works.

6 They shall speak of the might of your wondrous acts, *
   and I will tell of your greatness.

7 They shall publish the remembrance of your great goodness; *
   they shall sing of your righteous deeds.

8 You are gracious and full of compassion, *
   slow to anger and of great kindness.

9 You are loving to everyone, *
   and your compassion is over all your works.

10 All your works praise you, O God, *
   and your faithful servants bless you.

11 They make known the glory of your realm *
   and speak of your power,

12 That the peoples may know of your power *
   and the glorious splendor of your dominion.

13 Yours, O God, is an everlasting reign; *
   your dominion endures throughout all ages.

14 You are faithful in all your words *
   and merciful in all your deeds.

15 You uphold all those who fall; *
   you lift up those who are bowed down.

16 The eyes of all wait upon you, O God, *
   and you give them their food in due season.

17 You open wide your hand *
   and satisfy the needs of every living creature.

18 You are righteous in all your ways *
   and loving in all your works.

19 You are near to those who call upon you, *
   to all who call upon you faithfully.

20 You fulfill the desire of those who fear you; *
   you hear their cry and help them.

21 You preserve all those who love you, *
   but you destroy all the wicked.

22 My mouth shall speak your praise, O God; *
   let all flesh bless your holy Name for ever and ever.

Psalm 146

1 Alleluia! Praise God, O my soul! *
   I will praise God as long as I live;
   I will sing praises to my God while I have my being.

2 Put not your trust in rulers, nor in any child of earth, *
   for there is no help in them.

3 When they breathe their last, they return to earth, *
   and in that day their thoughts perish.

4 Happy are they who have the God of Jacob for their help, *
   whose hope is in their God;

5 Who made heaven and earth, the seas, and all that is in them; *
   whose promise abides for ever;

6 Who gives justice to those who are oppressed *
   and food to those who hunger.

7 God sets the prisoners free
   and opens the eyes of the blind; *
      God lifts up those who are bowed down;

8 God loves the righteous
   and cares for the stranger; *
      God sustains the orphan and widow,
      but frustrates the way of the wicked.

9 God shall reign for ever, *
      your God, O Zion, throughout all generations. Alleluia!

Thirtieth Day: Evening Prayer

PSALM 147

1 Alleluia! How good it is to sing praises to you, O God; *
   how pleasant it is to honor you with praise!

2 For you rebuild Jerusalem *
   and gather the exiles of Israel.

3 You heal the brokenhearted *
   and bind up their wounds.

4 You count the number of the stars *
   and call them all by their names.

5 Great are you and mighty in power; *
   there is no limit to your wisdom.

6 You lift up the lowly, *
   but cast the wicked to the ground.

7 We sing to you, Most High, with thanksgiving; *
   we make music to you upon the harp,

8 For you cover the heavens with clouds *
   and prepare rain for the earth;

9 You make grass to grow upon the mountains *
   and green plants to serve humankind.

10 You provide food for flocks and herds *
   and for the young ravens when they cry.

11 You are not impressed by the might of a horse; *
   you have no pleasure in human strength;

12 But you have pleasure in those who fear you, *
   in those who await your gracious favor.

13 Jerusalem will worship you, O God, *
   and Zion will praise your name.

14 For you have strengthened the bars of our gates *
   and have blest our children within us.

15 You have established peace on our borders *
   and satisfied us with the finest wheat.

16 You send out your command to the earth, *
   and your word runs very swiftly.

17 You give snow like wool *
   and scatter hoarfrost like ashes.

PSALM 147   239

18 You scatter your hail like bread crumbs; *
  who can stand against your cold?

19 You send forth your word and melt them; *
  you blow with your wind and the waters flow.

20 You declare your word to Jacob, *
  your statutes and your judgments to Israel.

21 You have not done so to any other nation; *
  to them you have not revealed your judgments. Alleluia!

Psalm 148

1 Alleluia! Praise God from the heavens; *
  sing praise in the heights.

2 Praise God, all you angels; *
  sing praise, all the heavenly host.

3 Praise God, sun and moon; *
  sing praise, all you shining stars.

4 Praise God, heaven of heavens *
  and you waters above the heavens.

5 Let them praise the Name of God, *
  by whose command they were created.

6 God made them stand fast for ever and ever, *
  and gave them a law which shall not pass away.

7 Praise God from the earth, *
  you sea-monsters and all deeps;

8 Fire and hail, snow and fog, *
  tempestuous wind, doing God's will;

9 Mountains and all hills, *
       fruit trees and all cedars;

10 Wild beasts and all cattle, *
       creeping things and winged birds;

11 Sovereigns of the earth and all peoples, *
       leaders and all rulers of the world;

12 Young men and maidens, *
       old and young together.

13 Let them praise your Name, O God, *
       for your Name only is exalted;
       your splendor is over earth and heaven.

14 You have raised up strength for your people
    and praise for all your loyal servants, *
       the children of Israel, a people who are near you. Alleluia!

Psalm 149

1 Alleluia! Sing to God a new song; *
       sing praise in the congregation of the faithful.

2 Let the people of Israel rejoice in their Maker; *
       let the children of Zion be joyful in their Monarch.

3 Let them praise God's Name in the dance; *
       let them sing praise with timbrel and harp.

4 God takes pleasure in the people *
       and adorns the poor with victory.

5 Let the faithful rejoice in triumph; *
       let them be joyful on their beds.

6 Let the praises of God be in their throat *
   and a two-edged sword in their hand,

7 To wreak vengeance on the nations *
   and punishment on the peoples;

8 To bind their rulers in chains *
   and their nobles with links of iron;

9 To inflict on them the judgment decreed; *
   this is glory for all God's faithful people. Alleluia!

PSALM 150

1 Alleluia! Praise God in the holy temple; *
   praise God in the firmament of power.

2 Praise God for every mighty act; *
   praise God's excellent greatness.

3 Praise God with the blast of the ram's-horn; *
   praise God with lyre and harp.

4 Praise God with timbrel and dance; *
   praise God with strings and pipe.

5 Praise God with resounding cymbals; *
   praise God with loud-clanging cymbals.

6 Let everything that has breath *
   praise God. Alleluia!

CPSIA information can be obtained
at www.ICGtesting.com
Printed in the USA
BVHW042002140222
628987BV00007B/36

9 781640 652057